From Maintenance To Outreach

From Maintenance To Outreach

Edited by Michael L. Roach
Outreach Ministries Commission
Missionary Office

REORGANIZED CHURCH OF JESUS CHRIST
OF LATTER DAY SAINTS
Herald Publishing House

Copyright © 1986
Herald Publishing House

All rights in this book are reserved. No part of the text may be reproduced in any form without written permission of the publisher, except brief quotation used in connection with reviews in magazines or newspapers.

Library of Congress Cataloging-in-Publication Data

Roach, Michael L.
   Outreach through neighborhood Bible study.

   1. Bible—Study. 2. Church group work. I. Title.
BS600.2.R57   1986   25947   86-9960
ISBN 0-8309-0456-5

Printed in the United States of America

6 5 4 3 2   90 91 92 93

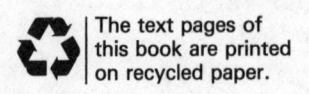

The text pages of this book are printed on recycled paper.

CONTENTS

Acknowledgments 6
Introduction 7
Missionary Outreach *Michael Roach* 17
    Charting a Course for Outreach 20
    Contemporary Christian Concert Series 32
    Developing Community Bible Study Groups .. 38
    Witnessing Support Groups 48
Zionic Relations Outreach *Robert E. Kent* 54
    Food Pantry 57
    Drop-In Center 62
    Stop Violence Campaign 67
    Congregational Peace Project 73
Outreach through Worship *Peter Judd* 75
    Visitors Day 78
    Community Worship Service 81
    Outreach Testimonies 83
    Visiting Speakers 85
    Worship beyond the Church 87
Outreach through Christian Education *Janet and David Chobar* 90
    Community Survey 94
    Training for Outreach 101
    Monthly Fun Activity Night 102
    Vacation Church School Ice Cream Social ... 107
Pastoral Care Outreach *Charles Mader* 111
    Orientation to Pastoral Evangelism 116
    Loss and Grief Workshop 120

    Community Course on Forgiveness........121
    Human Communication Skills Workshop...123
    God and I Communion Skills..............124
Pastoral Evangelism Recommended
    Reading List............................125
Stewardship Outreach *Lee Cummins*..........127
    Bridging the Connection Gap *Lee
    Cummins* 130
    Financial Planning for Singles
    Lee Cummins.........................136
    Emphasizing Wills Seminar *Claude
    Rains, Jr.*.............................140
    Recycling Project *Michael Roach*..........142

Acknowledgments

    There are many in the church who have given and continue to give extraordinary gifts of time, commitment, and talent to the kingdom-building venture. The contributing authors to this resource are of this group. Their "farsightedness" and desire to stay on the growing edge of God's ongoing work have made this resource possible.

Introduction

For many of us early impressions as youths in the church are of being loved by the Saints. We recall experiences of worship, study, and being cared for. These early caring relationships impressed upon us the value and meaning of sharing together in a "faith community."

The church is a faith community because it is a group of individuals who are bonded together by a common faith in the Lord Jesus. In this faith, individuals and the community grow and develop into powerful witnesses of God at work in the world. Communities of committed disciples work together to share the good news of God's grace to others.

This does not happen automatically. Witnessing and ministry are born out of a deep Christian commitment and a willingness to be directed by the Holy Spirit. Some disciples and faith communities grow and develop into "restoration" communities—communities committed to "preach the gospel to the poor...heal the brokenhearted...preach deliverance to the captives" (Luke 4:18) and to give "beauty for ashes, the oil of joy for mourning, the garment of praise for the spirit of heaviness" (Isaiah 61:3). Like Jesus, these communities are willing to grow, risk, and even die for the purpose of being reborn into more effective Christian disciples. Vital, living congregations remain in this cycle of growth, development, and death, seeking new ways for God to work with them and mold them into effective witnesses of divine love.

This resource uses a growth model fashioned after Jesus' example of birth, life, sacrifice, death, and resurrection. In this model, there are six stages.

Stage 1: *Birth and the Search for Meaning*

Individuals who gather together—mission groups, house churches, or new congregations—start at this stage. They come together to consider life and their place in it. They want to know what life means. Is there a purpose? If so, what is it, and what is their role in relation to it? Individuals share common concerns with one another. They bear testimonies and express hopes for the future. They seek mutual acceptance and support. They want to know what they can offer and where they will fit in. There is consideration of common heritage and tradition. Members of the congregation in this stage consider the extent to which they will commit themselves—their gifts, time, and energies—to the work of God. There may not as yet be a strong degree of commitment and support. Some members may take a "wait and see" attitude. As the congregation grows and members share experiences, this changes and the congregation begins to develop an identity and strong ties between members.

This first stage is illustrated in Jesus' time and in the early years of the Restoration. When Jesus gathered his disciples around him, they began to explore many things: God's call, their common ministry to the peoples of their time, what the coming of the Messiah meant, and how they each might respond. In the early years of the Restoration, Joseph Smith also gathered new disciples around him and bore his testimony of God's call. Together, Joseph and the first members of the church began to offer a witness to those with whom they came into contact. At the same time, they prepared for the growth and development of the young church.

Neither Jesus' disciples nor the early Restoration

communities remained in this stage. Truly dynamic and growing faith communities will move into stage two.

Stage 2: **The Sharing of Gifts**

In this stage, members of the congregation strengthen their commitments to Christ's ministry and to each other. A sense of permanency develops. Members plan to stay together in a mutually supportive and rewarding work. The search for meaning continues. The members of the congegation share in sacraments and gift giving which strengthens the foundation for their work together. The celebration of the Lord's supper, blessings, baptisms, worship (prayer, testimonies, singing, and preaching), education, and pastoral care are examples of these activities. A common purpose begins to unfold. Some new traditions are started which may serve as common reference points in the future. The increasing willingness to share concerns and gifts helps to create strong ties among the members and a sense of common purpose. Teamwork develops. Members are optimistic about the future and their relationship with each other. The congregation continues to grow and develop.

After Jesus died, the disciples who knew him personally had to decide what to do and how to do it. They prepared to carry on Jesus' ministry in his absence. The apostle Paul found ways to apply the teachings of Jesus in new environments. He worked with the Jerusalem church to plan for the spread of the gospel into non-Jewish cultures. He interpreted and applied gospel principles in new settings, thus starting new Christian traditions and paving the way for the continued growth and development of the young church.

In the Reorganization, the early Saints found it necessary to distinguish themselves from other denominations and movements. They emphasized such teachings as Zion, latter-day revelation, and the temple. Later, the Reorganization found it necessary to differentiate itself from Utah Mormonism. It sent missionaries into other countries and cultures, much as the apostle Paul had done many years before.

Congregational life in stage two can be rewarding and fulfilling. Ministry is being offered, relationships between members are mutually supportive, and participation in congregational activities is meaningful. But there is a tendency for many congregations to remain in this stage and not continue to grow and develop beyond the constraints of an internally focused ministry. In a sense, congregations in this stage begin to live only for themselves. They take care of their own needs and concerns—maintenance—and become increasingly unfamiliar and unresponsive to the needs of residents in the surrounding community. By placing themselves at the center of their concerns, they cease to be faithful to the gospel imperative to share the "good news" and go "into all the world."

Congregations in this stage must consciously decide to change. They must make a new commitment to Jesus' call to discipleship. When they do, they enter stage three.

Stage 3: **Confession, Repentance, and Renewal**

Congregations in this stage sense that they are expending too much energy on ministries which affect *only* themselves. They are settling for less than what God has called them to become—communities of faith engaged in the ministry of Jesus Christ in the world.

Congregations in stage two often fail to point beyond themselves to God and to a kind of ministry which is self-sacrificing and self-giving. Instead of becoming the embodiment of the symbols represented in the sacraments, many congregations accept them as ends in themselves. This is a form of idolatry. When they become aware of these human frailties and shortcomings, they also become aware of the need for confession and repentance. At this point the entire community confesses that it has forsaken the eternal call to become "new creations in Christ." Such communities are committed to continual change, risk, and growth. They trust God to meet them at each stage of their adventure with new revelations and new challenges.

The early Jerusalem church faced this dilemma when it wanted to withhold the gospel from non-Jews, believing that only those who were already Jews were ready for this new "Jewish Christianity." The apostle Paul perceived that God's call was for everyone and not just for those interested in an exclusive relationship with God.

In the early Reorganization, many Saints may have wished to keep the church for themselves, separating themselves physically and religiously from the surrounding communities. The experiences in Independence, Far West, Nauvoo, and in other cultures suggests that this was neither possible nor appropriate.

Congregations which reach this level of understnding soon realize that continued growth and development is necessary to be ultimately faithful to God's call. When this call is accepted and a renewed commitment is made, such congregations enter stage four.

Stage 4: **Embodiment**

As part of the process in stage three, congregations consider what they must do to grow beyond their internal, exclusive focus. They intentionally wish to "embody" the ministry of Jesus in their corporate and individual lives, as well as in their congregational programs.

In stage four the focus of the congregation shifts from maintenance to outreach. Programs within the congregation exist to develop and prepare the members for ministry in the surrounding community. These are programs of enablement. Programs of outreach are now the highest priority. Every potluck, worship service, and church school class has as a primary purpose the sharing of the good news of Jesus with those who have not heard it. New programs and new ministries produce new results. The congregation becomes an integral part of the community. It offers programs of vital interest to members and community residents. It deals with community-related issues and needs. It works with other community agencies and organizations as part of a network to provide healing, new life, hope, and opportunity to those who are "enmeshed in sin, longing to repent and follow [Christ]" (Doctrine and Covenants 153:9a). Congregations in stage four attempt to make their symbols real. They are the "good news." They are the body of Christ. They are the leaven and the salt.

As dynamic and necessary as stage four is, it is not the end. Jesus said "Whosoever will save his life, must be willing to lose it for my sake; and whosoever will be willing to lose his life for my sake, the same shall save it" (Luke 9:24). This means that a congregation chooses to sacrifice who and what it is now that others might find fulfillment in life. It surrenders its own will in obedience to the demands of Spirit-led Christian discipleship. Members put down their nets and follow Jesus. They risk who they are and what they do to serve others as the early disciples did. In a very real sense, they begin to live *not for themselves, but for others.* This decision leads to stage five in the congregational adventure.

Stage 5: ***Sacrifice and Death***

Needless to say, this is the ultimate faith walk for congregations. Very few ever achieve this stage because it requires complete surrender, dedication, sacrifice, and communion with God.

All attitudes, forms, structures, relationships, programs, and ministries are open to the insights gained from continuing revelation. Those which are imperfect—less than they could be—are replaced by new ones which will better enable the church to fulfill its calling for ministry in the world. The church and these elements transcend their current stage of growth and become "new creations" in Christ.

Because of our will to survive as communities, choosing to make this complete commitment is difficult. We wish to *preserve* instead of let go and move forward in faith. We would rather remain comfortable, stable, and permanent. By stopping short of this kind of commitment, we cannot glimpse or experience what may follow. But as our Christian heritage testifies, after death there is *resurrection*—new birth, new life, new hope, and new meaning. Congregations willing to take this step enter the final stage of growth and development as faith communities.

Stage 6: **Resurrection and Restoration**

These faith communities discover a deeper and more meaningful life. They do not exist to perpetuate themselves; rather, they live for others. They live almost as if existence itself did not matter as much as sacrificial service. Congregations in this stage are *eternal* as they embody and express a quality which is eternal and Christlike. Outreaching ministries of these congregations continually transcend—go beyond—who and what they are at any given time. They can offer Christ's redemptive love because they are living in salvation as the recipients and conveyors of God's grace. Finally, congregations which achieve this stage can offer a quality of life which is rare, as it follows the death of old forms and old ways, thus living at the growing edge of prophetic ministry.

Stage six communities continue to grow, develop, die, and be reborn in ever newer, more appropriate and effective forms of the body of Christ. This cycle exemplifies the process of "restoration" so dear to the church. This process calls the church and all members into a continual process of new life, new service, and new being.

Few historical faith communities have ever reached stage six. Few faith communities ever willingly choose *not* to exist in their present form for the purposes of assuming a more perfect form. The "confessional church" of Dietrich Bonhoeffer during World War II in Germany is one example. This faith community decided that it would rather not exist—would willingly sacrifice itself—to rid the world of Adolph Hitler. Thus, its members radically committed themselves to Jesus as the divine presence in the world, and to God, as the ultimate judge of

Hitler's actions. In their commitment and resulting actions, they chose to sacrifice themselves that other German Christians might live in a more humane society which recognized the worth of both Christian and Jew.

Other examples exist, but they are few. The age-old prophetic call to become new creations is continually before all disciples of Jesus Christ.

Members of a restoring congregation continually ask the questions Why do we exist as a body? What are God's purposes for us? What ministry can be offered? What gifts for ministry exist in the lives of our members and friends? What is the focus of current congregational programs and ministries? Are they primarily for those *inside* the congregation? Are we expending our energies and resources to minister to the needs of persons in the surrounding community?

The purpose of this resource is to encourage congregations to explore these questions. Each of the seven congregational areas are considered in light of this call. Each chapter includes a series of outreach activities which congregations committed to growth may incorporate into their overall program of ministry. To be sure, many congregations will not yet be ready for some of these outreach activities. But many will. Thus, these ministries may also serve as a challenge to enter fully into the faith community growth cycle, trusting that God will be present to sustain and enrich congregational life and ministry. These examples are ready to be put to use. They are practical and challenging, enabling and outreaching.

The contributors to this book express their confidence and hope that many congregations will accept the challenge to become growing, restoring communities, in harmony with the demands of total

Christian discipleship. It is their hope that many will "lay down their nets and follow Jesus," perhaps into horizons yet unknown and unexperienced.

                Robert E. Kent, director
                  Zionic Relations Office
                Michael L. Roach, director
                  Missionary Office

Missionary Outreach

By Michael L. Roach

"We have been amazed at the overwhelming response of the people in our neighborhood. As we have tried to reach out to them—the aged, the lonely, the winos, the floaters, even the young couples on limited incomes—we simply say, 'God cares, we care, and how can we help?'"

Evangelism is sharing the good news that God does care, and that through Jesus we can learn and practice the skills of caring and love. Our efforts to win persons to Christ is missionary outreach. The church has an exciting message to share. The message is filled with historical and present-day examples of restoration and renewal—calls to mission and unique purpose. However, the zeal and consistency of our outreach efforts often become bogged down in the day-to-day maintenance of schedules, programs, and services. We lose sight of the primary purposes of our discipleship—to win others to Christ.

The church as the body of Christ exists to be a living example of persons working together for the common purpose of creating a society based on peace and wholeness. Missionary outreach is the process of enlisting others in this cause. For this purpose, Christ's church must be a living church, vital and effective. There is no way a living church can exist in a vacuum. To be alive, it must join Jesus in the streets, move among those who long for purpose and meaning in life, and invite them to join their lives with others in life-giving ministry and service. This is missionary outreach. As the congregation embarks on this missionary journey, an amazing awareness will begin to grow. Persons will respond to the invitation to unite their lives with Christ and divine purposes—the Word of love becomes flesh—the claim of caring becomes reality in acts of giving and sacrifice.. The most profound and far-reaching personal witnessing will grow out of living congregations giving all there is to give for the renewal and redemption of others.

"Last year a friend and I planned a retreat. A husband and wife who attended were alcoholics—he had just been released from prison. The weekend was a turning point for them. After a year they testified that they had not taken a drink. But, more importantly, they had helped at least fifteen others come to Christ."

"After acquiring *Witnessing Support: Let Us Pray for One Another* from Herald House, I planned a party [for youths] at our farm home. By the third meeting members of the group were becoming very close to each other. Twila enjoyed Kelli's company. Kelli, in turn, reached out to Linda. Then Linda started bringing her younger sister, Wendy. Wendy reached out to Carrie and Shaun. Because Shaun comes, once in a while Ricky will come too. The girls got Keith to attend, and he invited Dustin. Dustin's cousins, Trevor and Scott, helped too. Glenda brought Tasha, and Tasha brought her little sister, Sherri. Twila reached out to Lou, and Lou brought Gretchen. This endeavor has started to resemble a spider's web. It just keeps expanding!"

This kind of outreaching ministry cannot be created or manipulated by programs packaged and sent out from headquarters. Resource helps become dust gatherers without the "Word become flesh" ministry of persons committed to Jesus Christ. Moving from maintenance to missionary outreach demands renewal of spiritual dedication—fresh awareness of the mission of discipleship we are called to. Renewal depends on persons giving their lives in obedience to God's love and grace. Many places throughout the church are experiencing a springtime "greening of the church." It is not because of programs and resources, but because of new life and purpose as the Saints open themselves to God's guiding presence and the ministry of Christ.

Missionary

Outreach Idea One:
Charting a Course for Outreach

When doctors, lawyers, builders, or mechanics begin their work, they first diagnose the conditions and needs which exist in order to accurately determine the work which needs to be done. They often use quantitative measurements and quantitative research to make qualitative judgments and plans for the job.

It is important for your congregation's members to diagnose where they are and where they have been in order to begin planning the active sharing of Christ's gospel for the future. One of the first and most important steps is to get an accurate picture of the congregation and the community in which you wish to minister. By following these suggested diagnostic steps, your congregation will be able to chart a course for long-range outreach based on existing and future needs of the members and the community. *Involve as many congregational members and friends as possible.* Widespread support is vital. The impact of these surveys and diagnostic efforts will be directly affected by the number of members and friends involved in obtaining them.

Step One—Ten-year Overview of Membership Statistics

  A. Design a graph following this example:
     Mountain Meadow Congregation
     1. On graph paper construct a scale from zero to twice your present membership. Each line on the vertical side of the example graph represents five members.

2. Along the bottom record the last ten years.
3. Use quarterly reports (the final or summary for each year), annual data reports, or other available records, to chart the *average* annual growth or decline of the following items. Record these in different colors.
    Red—Tithing Filers
    Blue—Baptisms
    Yellow—A.M. Worship Attendance
    Green—Church School Attendance
    Orange—P.M. Worship Attendance
    Brown—Midweek Service
    Black—Total Membership
4. Construct a table of percentages under the graph. Use the same color coding for easy identification. Divide the average of any category by the total membership for that year to arrive at the percentage.

    For example, the average attendance for P.M. services in 1975 was 29. The total membership for that year was 115. 29 divided by 115 is 25.2 percent of the total membership.

B. Calculate the rate at which your church increased over the past ten years. Here is an example:
    Current membership................138
    Membership ten years ago............115
    Ten-year increase....................23
The Mountain Meadow congregation grew from 115 by 12 new members:
    23 divided by 115 = 20 percent decade increase

Mountain Meadow Congregation
1975–1985 Expansion

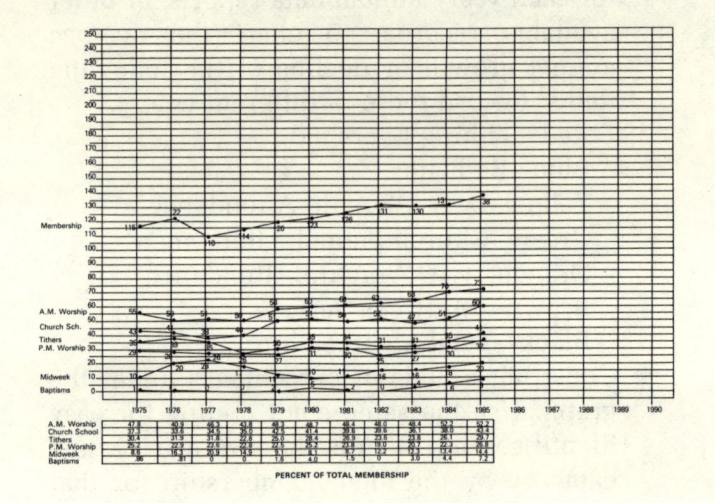

C. Children raised in a Christian community often join the church when they are old enough. This "natural increase" averages about 25 percent per decade. If your congregation increased by only 25 percent in the last decade, it is not really increasing at all in terms of persons who were previously unaffiliated with the RLDS church.

1. At first glance it would seem that the Mountain Meadow congregation is making steady growth. By natural increase the congregation should have reached 144 members. This means it is not keeping its natural increase nor adding new members.

2. Plot a natural increase line along your membership line. Take the membership of your

congregation for the first year, find 25 percent of that total, and add the two numbers following this example:

1975 Membership.... 115
25% of 115.......... +29 new members

Total membership which could be expected in 1985 by
natural increase......... 144

Mountain Meadow Congregation
1975–1985 Natural Increase

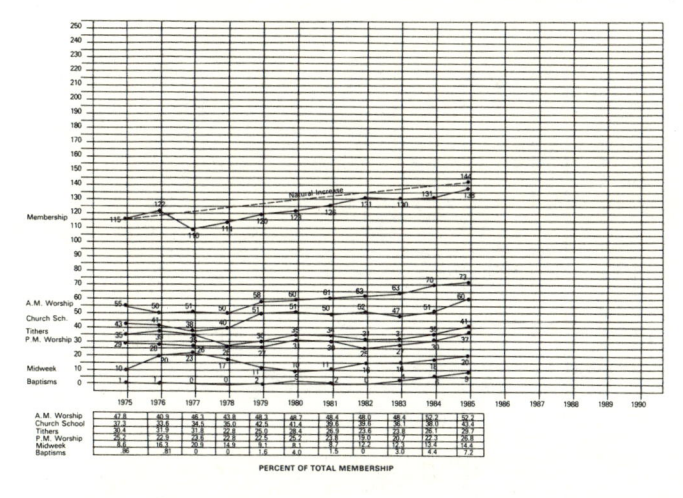

D. Analyze your congregation's decade expansion or decline.
   1. What kinds of leadership, programs, and ministries were taking place during the years of rapid expansion?
   2. What kinds of worship experiences were being offered?
   3. What conclusions can you draw from this ten-year picture?

E. Do not be discouraged if your graphs show decline. Use this information to make a new beginning with renewed commitment to take the good news of the gospel to those who have not yet heard it.

F. Project your congregation's natural increase for the next five years (½ of 25 percent based on your current membership).

**Mountain Meadow Congregation
1985–1990 Natural Increase Projection**

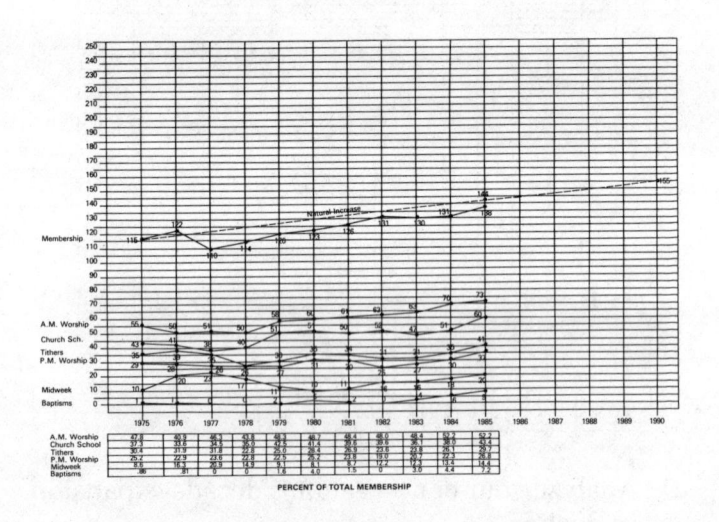

1985 Membership.........138
25% of 138 divided by 2 .... +17 new members
Total five-year membership
through natural increase..155

G. After prayer and consultation make a five-year "faith projection." A 50 percent decade

24

increase is a good place to start. Involve as many congregational members as possible.

Mountain Meadow Congregation
1985–1990 Five-Year Faith Projection

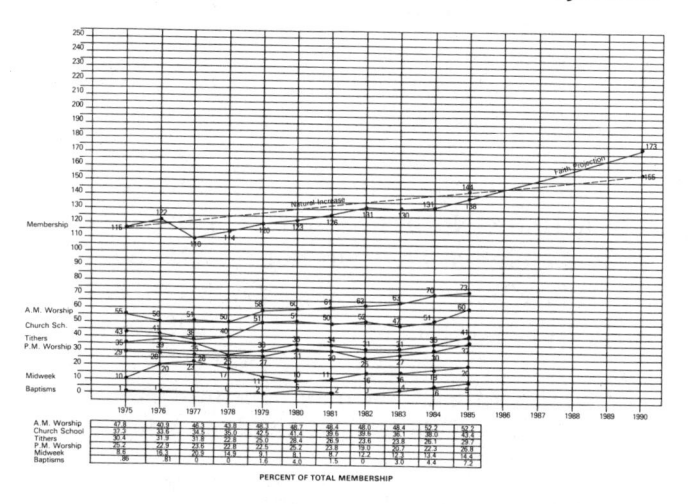

[Chart showing membership projection from 1975 to 1990, with Natural Increase and Faith Projection lines, reaching 173 by 1990 and 166 by natural increase. Data rows include A.M. Worship, Church School, Tithers, P.M. Worship, Midweek, and Baptisms shown as PERCENT OF TOTAL MEMBERSHIP.]

1985 Membership.........135
50% of 138 divided by 2.... +35 new members
Total five-year faith
 projection membership...173

Step Two—An Accurate Picture of Your Community

A. Obtain from any census bureau office the following information for the neighborhood or community in which you live:

   Number of people
   - Ages
   - Sex
   - Race
   - Marital status
   - Income level
   - Occupation
   - Educational level
   - Housing characteristics

25

The twelve census offices for the United States are

Area code/Number

Los Angeles, California......(213) 209-6612
Denver, Colorado...........(303) 234-5825
Atlanta, Georgia............(404) 881-2274
Chicago, Illinois............(312) 353-0980
Kansas City, Kansas.........(913) 236-3728
Boston, Massachusetts.......(617) 223-0226
Detroit, Michigan...........(313) 226-4675
New York, New York........(212) 264-4730
Charlotte, North Carolina....(704) 371-6144
Philadelphia, Pennsylvania...(215) 597-8313
Dallas, Texas...............(214) 767-0625
Seattle, Washington.........(206) 442-7080

Residents of Canada may call information for the number of *Statistics Canada* in your area.

B. Contact every Christian church in the area you wish to survey and ask them for their current total membership. For denominations practicing infant baptism obtain the number of members over the age of eight. Subtract this total Christian membership from the total population over the age of eight in the area you are surveying. This will give you a good idea of the number of non-Christian and unchurched persons in your community.

C. Mobilize your congregation for a door-to-door survey of your community. Use this form as an example.

COMMUNITY SURVEY FORM

1. Are you an active member of a local church?
   ___ Yes ___ No

   What faith or denomination?_____

2. If you were looking for a church, what would you look for?

   _____

   _____

   _____

3. What do you feel are two of your neighborhood's greatest needs?

   a. _____

   _____

   b. _____

   _____

4. If I were your pastor, what advice would you give me that would be of benefit to you?

   _____

   _____

   _____

   _____

5. Would you mind giving your name as part of this survey?
   ___ Yes ___ No

Name _____

Address _____

Date survey performed _____

Person filing the survey_____

Phone number_____

D. Enlist another group of congregation members to obtain the following information. Contact community churches, use the local telephone book, and ask every agency you contact questions concerning similar services available in the area.

EXISTING COMMUNITY SERVICES

Service or Program   **Location**

1. Child-care centers   _____

2. Literacy training/
   tutoring   _____

3. Counseling services   _____

4. Support Groups:

   Kind

   _____   _____

   _____   _____

   _____   _____

5. Transportation services

   Kind

   _____   _____

   _____   _____

6. Homemaker services _____
7. Emergency assistance _____
8. Legal services _____
9. Medical services _____
10. Financial services _____
11. Recreation programs _____
12. Hot meals/nutrition counseling _____
13. Other key agencies or services

        Name

_____ _____
_____ _____
_____ _____
_____ _____
_____ _____
_____ _____
_____ _____
_____ _____

Step Three—Plan for Outreach
  A. Compile a master list of all of the survey information.
     1. Observations concerning your congregation's expansion or decline over the last ten years
     2. The population profile from the census survey (numbers, ages, sex, income, and so on)

3. The number of unchurched persons in your community
4. Existing agencies and services
5. Expressed needs and opinions of community members

B. *As a congregation*, analyze the survey information in these terms:
1. The number of persons in your community who do not have a church home
2. The needs being expressed which are not being adequately met by other churches or agencies
3. The population makeup of your community (average age, race, income levels, number of children under the age of eighteen, number of young adults, churched, unchurched, and senior adults)

C. What ministries are suggested by the survey analysis?
1. What community services can your congregation extend to the area?
2. What kinds of worship and fellowship programs would appeal to the majority age range and racial makeup of your community?
3. What groundwork must be laid to begin moving the congregation from an inward focus, or maintenance mind-set, to a missionary focus of outreach to the unchurched of your community? Revival ministries may be needed to remind the Saints in your congregational family that "the truths of my gospel be proclaimed...and there are many

who will respond if you, my people, will bear affirmative testimony" and "as the church shall move forward in its great work, the fulfillment of prophecy may cause the Saints to tremble at the exhibition of divine power" (Doctrine and Covenants 153:9a, b, and 135:3b).

Missionary

Outreach Idea Two:
Contemporary Christian Concert Series

As your congregation gathers census statistics for the community you will possibly find that the majority of adults in your area are between the ages of twenty and forty. Of the two hundred and thirty million people in the United States, over eighty million are in this age range—one third of the total population. This is the first generation which grew up with television and rock music. Many in this age group will respond to contemporary Christian music, testimonies of Christ's healing grace, informal worship structures, and the call to be committed to a worthwhile cause.

Plan a series of contemporary concert events to be held on your church property, in the church, or within another available facility. Invite contemporary Christian bands and groups from your own congregation or community. Widely publicize the events with the intent of drawing a number of unchurched friends, relatives, and community residents—those persons who might otherwise feel uncomfortable in the traditional church setting and those who simply enjoy contemporary Christian music. Have teams of friendly greeters prepared to make contact with each visitor. Have church materials and tracts available for those who are interested. Provide ample opportunity for personal testimonies to be shared during the musical program. Create an atmosphere of fellowship and informal sharing.

Follow up on each concert event by contacting visitors with a call or personal visit. Express appreciation for their attendance. Extend an invitation for them to make your church their church home.

Explore the possibility of establishing a Contemporary Christian Center. The center could hold weekly services using contemporary Christian music, testimonies, and evangelistic preaching, with the intent of sharing the gospel of Jesus Christ with this particular age group of the unchurched.

Step One—Selecting Personnel and Preliminary Planning

A. At least six months before the event the missionary commissioner will meet with the pastor and the missionary commission to do the following:
   1. Determine which musical groups to invite.
      a. Local talent
      b. Other church groups
   2. Target the date of the first concert in conjunction with the availability of the music group(s), season, and community calendar.
   3. Determine the best setting for the concerts.
      a. Out of doors
      b. Inside the church
      c. Another community facility
   4. Develop a list of persons to organize and implement the various tasks involved.
      a. project coordinator—someone in the target age bracket who has a working knowledge of contemporary worship forms and music. This person will recruit volunteers to help as a project committee to be responsible for these tasks:
         (1) Contact and arrange for the musical group and testimonies

      (2) Develop the concert schedule and format
      (3) Arrange for any audiovisual presentations
      (4) Determine the kinds of equipment needed and communicate this information to the facilities coordinator.
      (5) Develop a tentative budget to submit to the missionary commissioner and pastor for approval.
  b. Facilities coordinator will recruit volunteers for the facilities committee to arrange for the following:
      (1) Staging
      (2) Lighting
      (3) Sound
      (4) Audiovisual equipment
      (5) Seating
      (6) Clean-up
      (7) A tentative budget to submit to the project coordinator
  c. Publicity and promotion coordinator will recruit volunteers as a publicity and promotion committee for the following tasks:
      (1) Arrange for the production and placement of posters and other advertisements in stores, newspapers, radio, and community locations.
      (2) Send a mass mailing and/or neighborhood distribution of fliers.
      (3) Place bulletin announcements encouraging every member to invite an unchurched friend or relative.
      (4) Develop a tentative budget to submit to the project coordinator.

d. Refreshments coordinator will recruit volunteers to work as a refreshment committee. They will do these things:
   (1) Select the food items to be made available.
   (2) Provide for eating utensils.
   (3) Develop a tentative budget to submit to the project coordinator.
e. Hospitality coordinator will organize a team of ten to twenty people to greet attendees:
   (1) Personally welcome *every* person attending the concert.
   (2) Distribute a handout advertising the next concert with a tear-off portion on which persons may write any special needs or concerns, name, address, and phone numbers (to be picked up during the concert).
   (3) Organize a follow-up committee to make personal phone calls, visits, or mail cards or notes to *every* visitor. (NOTE: This is an important facet of this outreach activity. There will be many who will respond to the caring and love extended by the disciples of Jesus Christ through this kind of consistent follow-up ministry, *particularly those who do not at present have a church family.*)
   (4) Arrange for a table to display tracts, books, pastoral care pamphlet series, and other literature.
   (5) Develop and distribute fliers listing the congregation's fellowship activi-

ties, calendar of events, and key phone numbers. If plans for a Contemporary Christian Center have been developed, take every opportunity to invite those present to attend. Describe the format of the services, and the Center's purpose—to share the gospel of Jesus Christ with persons of this age range in a contemporary and informal way.
  (6) Develop a tentative budget to submit to the project coordinator.

B. Once the coordinators have been chosen, the missionary commissioner will meet with these persons for planning which will include the following:
  1. Appraising them of their particular tasks
  2. Finalizing the date of the concert events
  3. Setting weekly or bi-weekly meeting dates for planning and preparation
  4. Setting a deadline for the submitting of tentative budget estimates

Step Two—Meet each week to coordinate efforts until the activity date.

Step Three—Execute plans for the Contemporary Christian Concert Series.

Step Four—Evaluate the series and the possibility of establishing a Contemporary Christian Center to evangelize the twenty-to-forty age group in your community. Contact the World Church Missionary Office or the Council of Twelve for information on successful Contemporary Christian Centers.

Step Five—Closely monitor the follow-up ministry. Loving, consistent follow-up will be the key to the success of the entire outreach efforts.

Step Six—Make plans for the use of these workshop training resources: *Personal Witnessing: The Challenge of Christian Discipleship, Witnessing Support Groups,* and *Nurturing New Members.*

Missionary
Outreach Idea Three:
Developing Community Bible Study Groups

The testimony of Jesus' life found in the Bible has been a foundation of strength and promise for two thousand years. We can hear the word of God and be moved. We can be told about the sure promises and biblical adventurers and become excited. But there is no substitute for experiencing the Word of God in personal and corporate study—discovering the meaning of the words for yourself.

Organizing a community Bible study group is an exciting way to introduce unchurched neighbors and friends to Christ. Friendships grow stronger. Lives are enriched. The Zionic principles of neighborliness and sharing are lived out.

Through an introductory program persons can be prepared to set up a Bible study group in their neighborhoods. The *primary* purpose of a community Bible study group is to fellowship in the Spirit of Christ—to share testimonies of God's grace and love. Out of this Christian sharing, opportunities may arise to offer invitations to unchurched neighbors and friends to make your church their church home, and to contribute insights found in our additional books of scripture.

Step One—The missionary coordinator will need to become familiar with the resources which are available for the formation of community Bible study groups.

    A. Contact Herald House for current resources on how to organize community Bible study groups. These resources suggest the use of several excellent Bible study guides which may also be ordered through Herald House. They are especially designed for small group Bible study and discussion.

1. Bible Study Series by the Christian Education Commission (Herald House)
   - Studies in Luke, Vol. 1
   - Studies in Luke, Vol. 2
   - Studies in Acts, Vol. 1
   - Studies in Acts, Vol. 2
   - Studies in Amos
   - Studies in Galatians
2. Fisherman Bible Study Guides
   - Genesis 1:25: Walking with God
   - Genesis 26:50: Called by God
   - David: Man After God's Own Heart (Volume I)
   - David: Man After God's Own Heart (Volume II)
   - Job: God's Answering to Suffering
   - Psalm: A Guide to Prayer and Praise
   - Proverbs and Parables: God's Wisdom for Living
   - Ecclesiastes: God's Wisdom for Evangelism
   - Amos: Israel on Trial
   - Jonah, Habakkuk, and Malachi: Living Responsibly
   - The God Who Understands Me: The Sermon on the Mount
   - Mark: God and Action
   - Luke: Following Jesus
   - John: Eyewitness

- Acts 1–12: God Moves in the Early Church
- Acts 13–28: God Moves in a Pagan World
- Romans: Made Righteous by Faith
- I Corinthians: Problems and Solutions in a Growing Church
- Ephesians: Living in God's Household
- Philippians: God's Guide to Joy
- Colossians: Focus on Christ
- Letters to the Thessalonians
- Letters to Timothy: Disciples in Action
- Hebrews: From Shadows to Reality
- James: Faith in Action
- Revelation: The Lamb Who Is the Lion
- Building Your House on the Lord: Marriage and Parenthood
- The Church: Pictures of Christ's Body
- Guidance and God's Will
- Higher Ground: For the Believer Who Seeks Joy and Victory
- Let's Pray Together
- Relationships
- Women Who Achieved for God
- Women Who Believe God

3. Navpress
   - Your Life in Christ
   - Spirit-Filled Christian
   - Walking with Christ
   - The Character of a Christian
   - Foundations for Faith
   - Growing in Discipleship
   - Our Home and Christ's Life
   - Leaders Guide
4. Neighborhood Bible Studies by Tyndale Press

- How to Start a Neighborhood Bible Study Group
- Acts
- Amos
- Choose Life
- The Coming of the Lord
- I Corinthians
- II Corinthians and Galatians
- Ephesians and Philemon
- Four Men of God
- Genesis
- Hebrews
- I John
- II John
- I John and James
- Luke
- Mark
- I Matthew
- II Matthew
- I and II Peter
- Philippians and Colossians
- Psalms and Proverbs
- Romans
- Set Free and They Met Jesus

5. The following is a sample page from the Fisherman Series:

answer is translated variously as, "Knew ye not that I must be about my Father's business?" or "Didn't you know that I had to be in my Father's house?" or "I was bound to be in my Father's house." The Greek phrase can be translated, "I must be involved in my Father's affairs," or "I must be among those people belonging to my Father." Luke 19:45/19:46 indicates the temple was considered God's house. So the straightforward answer of "Why were you looking for me? I had to be in my Father's house," seems the best. Jesus is referring to God as his heavenly Father in this instance and his earthly parents do not understand. Even Jesus' disciples did not understand at first. Luke records in Acts 1:14 that Mary was among the first believers.

Jesus remained under Mary and Joseph's care and obeyed them. And, like other young men, grew in body and mind.

4. *The group discusses the following questions.*
   a. Why is it important to Luke that ordinary people hear and accept the good news of Christ's birth? How does this reflect the situation at the time of the writing of Luke?
   b. What does the word *savior* mean?
   c. What are the Jewish traditions associated with the birth of a child? What relationship does Jesus have with these traditions? What does this relationship suggest about the nature of Jesus' childhood?
   d. Where in Luke can the theme of rejection be found? Do you think it was one of Luke's emphases? Why or why not? Compare these accounts in Luke with parallel passages in the other gospels.
   e. What difference does it make whether we believe Jesus developed like other boys physically and mentally or that he came into this world with greater knowledge and wisdom and only grew physically?
   f. Name the people who gave testimony of Jesus as the Messiah. What were their occupations?
   g. Describe the Passover celebration. Again, what relationship does Jesus have with this tradition? What does this suggest about the nature of Jesus' childhood?
   h. The author offers a number of translations for Luke 2:49. Do these various translations help you better understand the meaning of the original Greek? Why or why not?
   i. How does Luke's account of Jesus' activity in the temple differ from some popular conceptions of this event? What is the significance of that difference?

5. *The group reads the author's reflections on the passage.*
   The story of the birth of Jesus is well known to all Christians. We recite the familiar verses and sing of that wondrous night every year. December would not be the same unless we heard "Away in a Manger" or "Angels We Have Heard on High." Then we file away all those marvelous sights and sounds until next December, like the Christmas tree lights and baubles carefully packed in tissue paper and stored in a box in the attic.

   What would the story be like if Jesus were born tonight? Who would herald his birth? Who would be waiting in the sanctuary? If Luke were writing now, what would he say? And if we heard of Jesus' birth today, what would we think of it? Maybe no more or less than of the birth of any other child conceived before the parents were married.

   Jesus is our Messiah, so his birth inspires wonder and awe. This marvelous story of the very special birth of Jesus is accepted by faith because it is in our scriptures. We also need to accept Jesus' teaching, "Verily I say unto you, inasmuch as ye have done it unto one of the least of these my brethren, ye have done it unto me" (Matthew 25:41).

   The Christmas story is for all the year. We need to remember it with wonder, and marvel at a gracious God who would use the everyday, mundane events of life for special purposes. A child was born! The angels sang! The shepherds hurried to see! Simeon and Anna gave witness! The child grew!

   When we can no longer see the hand of God at work in our less-than-perfect world we are not living, or not looking! Rejoice and be glad for Jesus was born at Bethlehem.

6. *The group uses the following questions and activities to discuss the meaning of the text.*
   a. Share your first impressions of the passage with the other members of your group. What stood out as important to you? What was less important? Why?
   b. Use a Bible dictionary to look up the words *messiah, Christ, Jesus, anointed,* and *lord.* How does the meaning of these words bear on the Christmas story?
   c. Write the story of Jesus' birth in a modern setting.

Reprinted from *Studies in Luke* by Frances Easter, Herald House, 1985.

Step Two—Introducing Bible study groups
  A. The missionary coordinator will meet with the pastor to discuss the concept of community Bible study groups.

  B. The missionary coordinator and pastor will do the following:
   1. Set a date on which the concept of community Bible study groups can be introduced to the congregation (before or during a Sunday morning service in order to reach a maximum number of people).
   2. Set a date for a three-hour workshop during which interested members can explore the process of forming community Bible study groups and the resources available.
   3. Make plans for a bulletin insert describing community Bible study groups and announcing the introductory class for interested group organizers.

  C. Introduce the community Bible study group outreach effort to the congregation, announce the orientation time for those interested in becoming group organizers, and sign up interested persons before they leave the church that day.

Step Three—Group Organizers Orientation
  A. Most resources on organizing community Bible study groups cover several basic points. Use the orientation to discuss these important considerations which are summarized below. Encourage the group organizers to obtain a community Bible study group resource to study

on their own before beginning to organize their group.

B. Each of us is a missionary wherever we are. It is through our personal witnessing efforts and sense of call to Zionic community that the good news of a new and better life in Christ is shared with friends and neighbors.
   1. Many homemakers will respond to an opportunity to study informally the scriptures during the day while spouses and children are away at work and school.
   2. Many couples and single adults will respond to the opportunity to gather with other neighbors in a home one evening a week to explore the Bible.
   3. Very few persons feel knowledgeable about the Bible. For many, the scriptures seem threatening because of this unfamiliarity. Small group Bible *discussion* is an exciting way to break down these threatening barriers and open the doors to the good news of Christ.

C. The miracle of personal discovery
   1. Church goers have heard scripture-based preaching and teaching, but very few have ever read the Bible for themselves. Many unchurched persons have had *no* contact with scriptures as literature.
   2. There is no substitute for personal discovery. As persons read about Jesus and the prophets for themselves and allow the Holy Spirit to witness the truth and goodness

resident in those Christian principles, lives are changed and new possibilities are born.

D. Leadership styles
  1. Because of the importance of personal discovery and the influence of the Holy Spirit, it is important that the Bible study group be one of discussion and exploration and not lecture and teaching.
     a. Most study guides follow an approach in which the scripture is read and then questions are discussed which relate scripture to history and current life.
     b. Rotate leadership of the study group every week. This will ensure that no person becomes the "authoritative teacher." The group will remain as learners and explorers rather than as teacher and students.
  2. Keep the group's focus on the counsel and experiences contained in the Bible. Do not become overly distracted by doctrinal and theological issues. Each person will bring unique insights and understandings to the group. Accept and respect these insights and understandings without argument and debate. In this way participants will feel safe in offering their opinions and questions. The Holy Spirit will enable insight and understanding and the whole group will benefit if it will trust this process.

E. Group size
  1. Keep the group small enough to ensure intimate interaction and adequate opportunity for everyone to share.

    2. As the group grows it will become necessary to split and form other groups from time to time. This is a healthy principle of expansion and growth.

F. The cost of discipleship
   1. Because of the interaction and the presence of the Holy Spirit group members will become increasingly aware of their obligations as disciples of Jesus and as good neighbors.
   2. From time to time this Zionic principle will call group members to exercise godliness, patience, caring, and sharing in ways that they may have been reluctant to do before.

G. Invitation to new life
   1. Expect unchurched neighbors and friends to be touched by the love of Christ.
   2. Expect that these persons will begin to ask questions about the quality of life they are living.
   3. Be prepared to offer the kind of Christian counsel that will lead that awakening person to a new life in Jesus. At these points it is appropriate to invite the friend or neighbor to come to church with you and explore an expanding experience of Christian fellowship and love.
   4. Expect that some of the group members will become more active in their own denomination.
   5. Expect that some group members will not be interested in expanding their Christian fellowship beyond the neighborhood group.

Step Four—Follow-up
- A. The missionary coordinator will maintain close contact with the group leaders to ensure that they are equipped with the needed resources.

- B. Meet with the group leaders monthly to lend support and guidance to the Bible study efforts.

- C. Plan prime-time Sunday opportunities for group leaders and members to share testimonies arising from the group experiences.
  1. As lives are changed and new disciples are added to the church the news will spread.
  2. New groups will begin to appear and the process will expand.

- D. Repeat this entire introduction and orientation process every nine to twelve months.

Missionary

Outreach Idea Four:
Witnessing Support Groups

Jesus said, "The harvest truly is great, but the laborers few; pray ye therefore the Lord of the harvest, that he would send forth laborers into his harvest.... Heal the sick that are therein, and say, The kingdom of God is come nigh unto you" (Luke 10:2, 9).

Challenge your congregation to form several witnessing support groups. These small groups will prayerfully support each other as they answer Jesus' call to take their testimonies of God's redemptive love to others who have not heard the good news.

Witnessing support groups can bring new life and the vital mission of Christ back into focus for your congregation. It is in these kinds of personal witnessing efforts that disciples discover that Jesus' promise to go before them is true, and persons can come alive through God's saving grace.

Step One—Preliminary planning

A. The missionary coordinator will obtain a copy of *Witnessing Support Let Us Pray for One Another*. Become familiar with the witnessing support group concept. A copy of the leader's guide and participants' workbook may be borrowed from the Missionary Office in the Auditorium for initial familiarization. The witnessing support group kit, which contains one leader's manual, ten participants workbooks, and twenty-five invitational brochures can be purchased through Herald House.

B. In consultation with the presiding elder the missionary coordinator does the following:
   1. Sets the date on which a three-hour workshop can be held for orientation of potential witnessing support group leaders.
   2. Selects a Sunday morning closely following the orientation class to hold a witnessing service during which the witnessing support group concept can be introduced to the congregation.
   3. Plans a series of worship services focused on personal witnessing which will lead up to the culminating witnessing service and introduction of the witness support group concept.

Step Two—The missionary coordinator will invite several men and women of the congregation to become witnessing support group leaders.
   A. Briefly explain to each individual the witnessing support group concept.

   B. Invite each person to attend the orientation activity to prepare for leadership of a witnessing support group.

Step Three—Witnessing support group leader orientation
   A. Purchase a complete witnessing support group kit from Herald House.

   B. Once again briefly explain the witnessing support group concept.

C. Familiarize the group leaders with leader's handbook and participants' workbook.
   1. Explain the easy-to-follow format. Assure the potential leaders that the resource has been written to be easily followed by anyone, whether experienced in small group leadership or not.
   2. Briefly touch on the topic of each of the six support group meetings. Explain the goal of each of those group meetings.
   3. Model a group meeting by taking the leaders through one of the sessions as if they were a small witnessing support group.

Step Four—Witnessing service
A. This witnessing service should be the culmination of several Sunday morning and Wednesday evening experiences that have had personal witnessing as their focus. Provide copies of the invitational brochures for each member of the congregation as part of a bulletin insert or toward the end of the witnessing service. Quantities of these brochures can be purchased from Herald House or may be photocopied for congregational use.

B. Suggested format for the witnessing service
   1. Testimonies by three or four individuals, rather than a sermon on witnessing, should be the focus. These testimonies can be by persons recently converted because of witnessing efforts or those who have been actively involved in personal witnessing and who can testify of the good that has come from those efforts.

2. Intersperse these testimonies with ministry of vocal and instrumental music, choral scripture readings, appropriate poetry, and other worship expressions.
3. Allow enough time toward the end of the service to introduce the congregation to the witnessing support group concept.
    a. In two to four minutes, briefly explain the concept of a witnessing support group.
    b. Hand out the witnessing support group invitational brochures (or have them as part of the bulletins).
4. Invite the witnessing support group leaders to stand and be recognized by the congregation.
5. Provide opportunity for interested congregational members to sign up for a witnessing support group before they leave.

Step Five—Immediately following the witnessing service the missionary coordinator will meet with witnessing support group leaders to make plans for the first set of meetings.
A. Take the names of congregational members interested in becoming part of a witnessing support group and assign groups as geographically compact as possible.

B. Encourage the group leaders to contact each of their group members within the next two to three days.

Step Six—Getting started
A. The group leaders will contact each member of

51

their group to determine what day or evening of the week would be best for the group to meet.

B. Set the date, time, and place for the first group meeting.

C. Start witnessing!

Step Seven—Follow-through
   A. The missionary coordinator will meet regularly with the group leaders for encouragement and support.

   B. In consultation with the presiding elder, plan to provide opportunities for group members to share testimonies concerning the fruits of their witnessing efforts. These efforts are the heart of what God has called us to do—take the gospel to all those who have not heard. Because of the importance of this task, "prime-time" Sunday opportunities should be provided for the good news to be shared with the congregation. This will continually encourage the congregation to greater personal witnessing efforts as well as ensure the organization of a growing number of witnessing support groups.

Step Eight—Starting more groups
   A. As the groups complete the six support meetings they can choose to disband. Each member can become a leader of another witnessing support group.

   B. The group can continue for a time. Another resource is available from Herald House titled

Witnessing Support: Sharing the Gospel with Friends. This resource is a supplement to *Let Us Pray for One Another.* It provides an additional seven sessions.

Step Nine—Begin new witnessing support groups every six to nine months.

Zionic Relations Outreach
By Robert E. Kent

"Our congregation is situated in a prime area for youth. Children walking to and from school pass the church building every day. The apartments near the church are full of children. This was a great opportunity for the body of Christ to make an impact in the community. We took advantage of it. We started an after school 'drop-in center.' It includes recreational activities, crafts, and tutoring on certain subjects. It has been a good way for our congregation to help the youth in our area. Eventually, we started classes for nonmembers. Some of the parents came to church with children from the center. We had no idea what the results would be!"

"Our congregation was looking for some way to make a contribution to the neighborhood. So we started a food pantry. Various foodstuffs are collected each Sunday from the members of the congregation. In addition, we have someone who calls supermarkets each week to inquire about excess food that has not been sold. We then arrange to pick up the food and distribute it to community residents. We also contribute food to the local food bank for wider distribution. This is our way of demonstrating our care and concern for the hungry in the community."

These two examples illustrate Zionic relations. They demonstrate a congregation's efforts to bring the church and the community closer together. In this process the resources within the church—facilities, skills, time, service, caring—are used to address needs in the surrounding community. The relationships which result can help to strengthen both the church body and the community. Artificial barriers are removed, common misconceptions about the church and the community dissolve, and the church benefits from the service it gives in ways not often anticipated.

The Reorganized Church of Jesus Christ of Latter Day Saints has long been concerned about the "cause of Zion." Quite often, this cause has been viewed either as the exclusive domain of the church or as something which would happen in the future. But the cause is an urgent one. If it has any importance whatsoever, if persons living in our communities need the church's ministry to improve their lives then the church must become "anxiously engaged" in efforts to improve the quality of life around it.

The church cannot do this alone, nor should it try. Rather, its members should look for ways to pool its resources and thereby "network" with other community organizations. In this way, limited resources can expand to address common concerns and meet common needs. Such an approach is not only good stewardship, but common sense as well. Members of the congregation can volunteer for community programs. Community organizations can use church facilities for special events or activities. The congregation then becomes a "leaven" in the life of the surrounding community.

To be sure, this process is neither easy nor accomplished instantly. It demands large amounts of commitment, perseverance, time, and energy. After a period of internal growth in the congregation—study, skill development, planning, organization, celebration, and consecration—a congregation will be ready to reach out beyond the walls of the church into the lives of community residents. This kind of outreaching ministry—Zionic relations—is an investment, a planting of sorts. It may take time to see results. But if there is sufficient growth and internal development followed by a strong commitment to outreaching ministry, the church can expect a good harvest.

Behold, the field is white already to harvest, therefore, whoso desireth to reap, let him thrust in his sickle with his might, and reap while the day lasts.... Yea, whosoever will thrust in his sickle and reap, the same is called of God.
—Doctrine and Covenants 6:2a, b.

The program models which follow are but a few suggestions for Zionic relations ministry. A variety of factors will determine what any one congregation will do and how it will do it: its stage of growth and development, its perception of God's call for ministry in the surrounding community, and the amount and kind of resources available for ministry, to name a few. Prior to understanding a project of any kind, a congregation should be exposed to *Zion: The Church in Community,* a multi-media workshop kit designed for congregations to consider how to engage in Zionic relations programming. After going through this workshop and reflecting on the above concerns, a congregation may consider the unique response it will make to God's call to be engaged in "the cause of Zion."

The *Servant Ministry Handbook* (Herald House) contains helpful suggestions for congregations involved in specific programs of outreach.

Zionic Relations

Outreach Idea One:
Food Pantry

Hunger is not just a problem overseas. It exists in our own communities. As government programs are reduced or eliminated, someone must step in to take up the slack. Many churches throughout the country have established food pantries where a variety of foodstuffs are collected and stored in the church for distribution to community residents. Some congregations collect the food for transfer to the local community food bank. Others collect, store, and distribute food in the communities surrounding the church. Seldom-used room in the church can be designated as the pantry storage area and equipped with shelves to handle the volume of food to be collected. Appoint someone to contact local food sources—supermarkets, convenience stores, restaurants—and arrange to collect food for the pantry. Make regular collections. Someone else can arrange the storage area, check the inventory periodically, and handle the restocking efforts. A third person can direct food distribution, including publicity for the pantry in the community. With three to five committed persons, a congregation can have an impact on hunger in the immediate community.

Step One—Preliminary Planning

Several months prior to collecting the first food, the Zionic relations commission will meet with the pastor to plan for a food pantry:
    A. Evaluate the need for a food pantry in the community.

B. Develop a project proposal for consideration by the congregation.

C. Write job descriptions for those who will serve on the project.

D. Establish a project budget.

E. Consider methods of networking with other community agencies.

F. Consider methods of promoting and publicizing the pantry inside and outside the church.

G. Designate the storage space in the church for the pantry.

Step Two—Developing the Project
The Zionic relations commission will take these steps:
  A. Arrange for converting the designated space into a pantry.

  B. Recruit persons for the following tasks:
    1. Contact local food sources and do the collecting.
    2. Organize the storage area and keep up the inventory.
    3. Distribute the food to community residents or to the local food bank.

  C. Provide those recruited with job descriptions.

  D. Establish a target date for opening the pantry.

E. Promote the effort inside and outside the church.

F. Contact appropriate community agencies to determine how to coordinate efforts.

Step Three—Beginning to Serve
A. When the planning and development of the project is complete, those persons recruited may begin the operation of the food pantry.

B. The Zionic relations commissioner's duties will be as follows:
   1. Coordinate the efforts of those running the pantry.
   2. Publicize and promote the ongoing operation of the pantry.
   3. Keep in touch with those serving to monitor their efforts, encourage them, and assist in resolving any difficulties.
   4. Coordinate with other community agencies to avoid any duplication of service.
   5. Coordinate periodic evaluations of the project.

C. Duties of the food collector
   1. Make the initial contacts with potential food sources to discover what kinds of foods are available.
   2. Make arrangements to collect foods on certain days and in certain quantities.
   3. Pick up food at the designated places and times.
   4. Coordinate these pickups with the storage coordinator.

D. Duties of the storage coordinator
   1. Label the shelves in the pantry for the appropriate foods.
   2. Establish the proper inventory levels for each category.
   3. Coordinate the pickups with the food collector.
   4. Coordinate the distribution of foodstuffs with the distribution coordinator.
   5. Participate in periodic project evaluations.

E. Duties of the distribution coordinator
   1. Coordinate the distribution with the storage coordinator to ensure that sufficient numbers of certain foodstuffs are available for distribution.
   2. Distribute foods to community residents, ensuring that there is no overlap with other community services.
   3. Keep the pastor and the Zionic relations commissioner informed as to the progress of the project.
   4. Meet with the pastor, others serving on the project, and the Zionic relations commissioner to periodically evaluate the functioning of the project.

Step Four—Periodic Evaluations

The pastor, Zionic relations commissioner, commission members, and those who serve on the project should meet periodically to evaluate progress and to make necessary adjustments.

Step Five—Project Completion

At the time the project goals are met (unless it is on-

going), all those involved in coordinating and servicing the project will meet for a final evaluation session.
  A. Evaluation forms or questionnaires should be distributed to those having contact with the project. Tabulate the results and review prior to the meeting.

  B. A wrap-up checklist should be formulated and used for this session.

  C. Key task to accomplish
    1. Pay outstanding bills and close out the budget.
    2. Plan a closing service of worship or recognition for the congregation.
    3. Write necessary letters or reports (e.g., to jurisdictional officers, community agencies or leaders, and selected supporters outside the church).
    4. Thank all those who helped.

Zionic Relations

Outreach Idea Two:
Drop-In Center

In recent years, "latch-key children" have been of increasing interest and concern in our communities. Latch-key children are those who return home from school to an empty house, either because they have no sisters or brothers or because the parents are still at work. Many congregations are located in "high traffic areas," posing one of many safety hazards for the children and youth from the neighborhood. To address these concerns, establish a "drop-in" center for latch-key children. Other children and youth will also have a place to go after school.

A drop-in center may include recreation programs with both individual and team sports, classes on certain hobbies and crafts, and tutoring opportunities. Invite retired persons and parents who do not work outside the home or who have flexible afternoon hours, to volunteer their time and talents. High school or college students can lend their academic or athletic skills after school. This program will also provide valuable contact with the parents, many of whom will be unchurched and very interested in what the church is providing for their children.

This project will break down some artificial barriers which often exist between the church and community residents and between the church and other community agencies. It may fill a gap in community services or supplement those already existing.

Step One—Preliminary Planning

Several months prior to opening the center, the

Zionic relations commissioner will meet with the pastor and the Zionic relations commission to make the following decisions:
A. Determine the feasibility of a drop-in center.
   1. Contact other churches and community agencies.
   2. Survey the community to determine interest.
   3. Determine how many youth and children live close to the church (see missionary outreach idea 1).
   4. Identify those church members and community residents who will volunteer their time and talents.

B. Establish a target date for opening the center.

C. Determine what facilities and resources will be necessary and available for use.

D. Consider the list of persons who are willing and able to serve on a regular or part-time basis.

E. Choose a project coordinator.

F. Develop a project proposal for the congregation to consider and approve.

G. Establish a project budget.

H. Write job descriptions for those who will serve on the project.

I. Formulate a publicity and promotion plan.

Step Two—Developing the Project

The Zionic relations commission will do the following:

A. Identify persons to accumulate the necessary resources and prepare the facilities for the project.

B. Recruit persons to serve as coaches, teachers, tutors, assistants, and other resource persons.

C. Provide those recruited with job descriptions and support.

D. Promote the effort inside and outside the church.

E. Develop an operations policy to define each function of the center—what sports will be offered, how they will be run, which subjects for tutoring will be offered, what crafts will be taught, and what rules of behavior will be enforced and how.

F. Contact city departments for information concerning special permits or ordinances.

G. Contact those who were responsive during the community survey to inform them of the center's opening date.

Step Three—Beginning to Serve

A. When the planning and development of the project is complete, persons recruited to serve in the center may begin their responsibilities.

B. Duties of the project director
   1. Coordinate the overall program.
   2. Publicize and promote the ongoing operation of the center.
   3. Keep in touch with those serving—monitor their efforts, encourage them, and assist in resolving any difficulties.
   4. Ensure that the necessary resources are available.
   5. Coordinate periodic evaluations of the project.

C. Duties of the recreation coordinator
   1. Set up various activities and recruit persons to assist in coaching or playing with the children and youth.
   2. Ensure that the proper equipment is available and used safely.
   3. Take care of scheduling for team sports.
   4. Work with other community recreation programs to arrange "inter-program" competition and events.
   5. Participate in periodic project evaluations.

D. Duties of the crafts coordinator
   1. Accumulate the necessary resources and materials for the classes.
   2. Recruit persons to assist.
   3. Participate in periodic project evaluations.

E. Duties of the tutoring coordinator
   1. Accumulate the necessary materials for each subject to be tutored.
   2. Recruit persons to assist with various subjects or study time.

3. Be in touch with the parents and schools to determine actual needs and to report progress.
4. Participate in periodic project evaluations.

Step Four—Periodic Evaluations

The pastor, Zionic relations commissioner, commission members, and those serving on the project should meet periodically to evaluate progress and to make necessary adjustments. Invite parents with children active in the project to participate.

Step Five—Project Completion

When the project goals are met (unless it is ongoing), all those involved in coordinating and serving should meet for a final evaluation and wrap-up session.
  A. Distribute evaluation forms or questionnaires to all those having contact with the project—coaches, teachers, tutors, students, youth, parents, members of the congregation, commission members. Tabulate the results before the meeting.

  B. Formulate and use a wrap-up checklist.

  C. Some key tasks to accomplish
    1. Close out the budget and resolve outstanding expenses.
    2. Plan and offer a formal closing event.
    3. Write reports and/or letters to key persons in the church and the community.
    4. Ensure that the facilities and resources are returned to proper condition and places.

Zionic Relations

Outreach Idea Three: Stop Violence Campaign

Domestic violence has become a matter of increasing concern in recent years. Spouse abuse and child abuse are two manifestations of this program. Deaths have resulted from years of continuous and violent abuse. The physical dimensions of the problem are often readily apparent. But it is difficult to determine the extent of trauma and psychological harm done to those subjected to domestic violence.

Many churches have begun to support those directly affected by the problem by participating with other organizations in efforts of education and advocacy. They have helped to create shelters for the victims. Quite often, people we already know are caught up in this crisis. They need a special ministry of caring, empathy, counseling, and continual support.

The following program model will prove helpful to a congregation wishing to participate in a "stop violence campaign."

Step One—Preliminary Planning

Several months prior to the active involvement of the congregation in this campaign, the Zionic relations commissioner will meet with the pastor and the Zionic relations commission to do the following:

A. Formulate a project proposal for the congregation to consider.

B. Survey the community to determine what is already being done in this area and use this information to determine the projected level and nature of congregational involvement.

C. Establish a target date for presenting the project proposal to the congregation.

D. Develop a step-by-step skeleton plan and budget for the program.

E. Choose who will coordinate the program and those who will be asked to serve.

F. Write job descriptions for those serving in the program.

G. Develop a plan for promotion and publicity for inside and outside the church.

H. Consider possible means for evaluating the effectiveness of the campaign.

Step Two—Developing the Program

The Zionic relations commission (or program committee) will meet to complete these tasks:

A. Review the project proposal and job descriptions.

B. Consider each aspect of the program and assign responsibilities for various parts.

C. Recruit additional persons to help if necessary.

D. Determine how the program will be promoted and publicized inside and outside the church.

E. Identify an area inside the church that will be used for information and materials about the campaign.

F. Establish a system for working with other organizations and agencies involved in this problem.

G. Plan future meetings.

H. Develop the means to properly evaluate the program during its operation and at its conclusion.

Step Three—Beginning to Serve
A. Duties of the program coordinator
   1. Coordinate the overall program.
   2. Keep in touch with those serving—monitor their efforts, encourage them, and assist in resolving any difficulties.
   3. Represent the program to the congregation and the community.
   4. Coordinate periodic evaluations of the program.
   5. Monitor and maintain the program budget.

B. Duties of the issue analyst
   1. Research the extent of the problem, both nationally and locally, in terms of existing support structures for victims, laws and regulations governing abusers, and organizations already involved in solutions to the problem.
   2. Contact key community and national leaders about the issue such as agency heads, legislators, and other researchers.
   3. Prepare and deliver reports to the program committee and the congregation.

4. Assist in efforts to educate and inform the congregation about the problem.
5. Be in touch with other community and national agencies and organizations to give and receive information.
6. Follow guidance provided by the program committee on follow-up research and analysis.
7. Participate in periodic program evaluations.

C. Duties of the community network coordinator
1. Contact other community agencies or churches to determine what is already known and being done about the issue and how the congregation may cooperate with them.
2. Attend meetings and functions of other agencies and organizations to discover points of overlap or gaps in ministry.
3. Report back to the program committee and the congregation on progress.
4. Participate in periodic program evaluations.

D. Duties of the publicity and promotion coordinator
1. Promote the work of the congregation and others involved in the campaign, both inside and outside the church.
2. Identify key successes and problems needing further attention and work.
3. Work with the local media to publicize key events and other newsworthy items.
4. Participate in periodic program evaluations.

E. Duties of the program activity coordinator
   1. Assist in the planning and coordination of each event held in the church as part of the program.
   2. Assist in the planning of events in which the congregation participates, but not held at the church.
   3. Ensure that the facilities are adequately prepared for the event and accumulate necessary resources.
   4. Recruit persons necessary to assist with events.
   5. Coordinate events with other program staff persons to cover gaps and avoid conflicts.
   6. Participate in periodic evaluation sessions.

Step Four—Periodic Evaluations

The pastor, Zionic relations commissioner, commission members, and those participating in the campaign will meet periodically to evaluate the success of the campaign and make necessary adjustments. These occasions may be used to refocus or redirect existing efforts.

Step Five—Project Completion

At the conclusion of the project (unless it is ongoing), all those from the congregation involved in the coordination and service in the campaign should meet for a final evaluation and wrap-up session.

A. Distribute evaluation forms or questionnaires to all key persons and tabulate the results prior to the meeting.

B. Formulate and use a program wrap-up checklist to avoid leaving loose ends.

C. Be sure to accomplish the following tasks:
 1. Close out the budget and pay outstanding bills.
 2. Plan and offer a closing event—supper, recognition, or worship service—and invite key persons in the community who participated in the program or the campaign.
 3. Write final reports and letters to key persons.
 4. Return facilities and resources to their proper condition or place.

Zionic Relations

Outreach Idea Four:
Congregational Peace Project

The issues of war and peace have become of increasing concern in the last few years. The nuclear arms race continues unabated. The increasing militarization of Central America includes gross human rights violations and the murder of innocent men, women, and children. So much money is being spent on arms that other sectors of the Central American economies are deprived, contributing to widespread disease and poverty. The Middle East remains a volatile and unstable area of the globe, with different political and religious factions vying for power. These are only representative of other armed conflicts and the need for peace and reconciliation all over the world.

In 1982, the assembled delegates of the World Conference passed two resolutions: "Nuclear Disarmament" and "Peace." These two resolutions, constituting the official position and guidance of the church on these matters, contain important challenges to the members of the church to become active in peacemaking efforts throughout the world. The following excerpts are of particular significance.

> We, as a church, share the responsibility for world conditions.... We express our sense of responsibility in such ways as:
>
> A. Calling on persons to accept their stewardship over God's creation.
>
> B. Encouraging persons to adjust their personal lifestyles toward the elimination of waste, greed, and insensitivity.

C. Committing our resources in the pursuit of peace, justice, reconciliation, and human development.

D. Encouraging individuals to support leaders who are promoting peace.

E. Speaking out against human inequity wherever and whenever it is found.

We, as a church, oppose all forms of destructive violence, such as national and international conflict, war, withholding of food, terrorism, and mental and physical abuse.
—WCR 1177, Peace

Resolved, That we, as a church, through appropriate administrative representatives at every jurisdictional level (world, national, regional, district, stake, pastoral unit) shall inform the appropriate governmental officials of the need for responsible reduction and eventual elimination of nuclear armaments; and be it further...

Resolved, That we, as a church, join with other organizations that are constructively promoting a reduction of instruments of mass destruction.
—WCR 178, Nuclear Arms Reduction

Follow the program model offered in outreach activity 3 to fulfill the intent of these two resolutions. Congregations can pursue this to the extent of their commitment and available resources.

Outreach through Worship
By Peter Judd

In our worship we celebrate God's presence among us. We give thanks for life's blessings and for the privilege of gathering together as the people of God. Worship provides nurture, strength, and inspiration. It is the expression of the body of Christ gathered in one place. We view worship as that which equips us to be Christ's disciples in the world after we leave the comfort of the church sanctuary. But how often do we think of our congregation's worship services as opportunities for outreach?

Another way to pose this same question is to ask, How frequently do we invite our nonmember friends, relatives, or neighbors to worship with us? or How often do we leave a service of worship thinking that the service would have been meaningful to friends had they been present? Our truthful response to these questions is probably "Not frequently enough."

A major change in attitude concerning congregational worship may be necessary if we are to see it as a valuable means of outreach. We must *believe* that worship can be a bridge between the church and the communities in which we live. We must have confidence that our worship *will* have meaning for persons who have not been regular members of the church fellowship.

In order to have positive expectations about worship's potential for outreach, we need to plan and experience quality worship on a regular basis. We cannot expect nonmember friends to be more excited about and ministered to by worship than we are ourselves. For worship to be an effective means of outreach it must demonstrate a depth and vitality that emerge from the lives of the members.

The following questions can help us assess the ways in which our worship can become a more effective vehicle for outreach.

1. How many persons whose names appear on the congregational roles attend worship services once per month or less? Which regular attenders are friends of these persons and are in the best position to encourage them to resume active worship attendance?
2. Why do infrequent attenders rarely come to worship? If you do not know for sure, ask them. How might your congregation's worship be planned to better meet these persons' needs?
3. How many nonmembers have attended worship services in your congregation during the last year? Have they been contacted with an invitation to return? How can follow-up be made more effective?
4. What specific parts of your congregation's worship services over the last three months have had specific appeal for nonmembers? What specific parts have excluded them? How can the former be used more frequently and the latter less often?
5. Has the worship commission or others who have responsibility for worship planning recently discussed how your congregation's worship services can become a more effec-

tive method of outreach? If not, when can such an exploration be scheduled?
6. How frequently in your congregation's worship services is the gospel brought to bear on the real-life situations of the worshipers? How can this be made to happen more often?
7. Which of the commonly used forms of worship are most in need of revitalization in your congregation? Prayer? Scripture reading? Preaching? Hymn singing? How can these be improved through the offering of skill-development opportunities to those who serve as worship leaders?
8. What opinions would a nonmember likely form about your congregation after attending a worship service? What is communicated by (a) the actions of worship, (b) the words spoken, (c) the way the worshipers are seated—spread out or or close together, (d) the way members relate to each other before, during, and after worship, and (e) the way members relate to visitors?

These questions may help us reflect on the extent to which our worship currently serves the outreach interests of our congregations. They can also aid us in identifying possible areas for change.

The following program ideas present specific ways that a congregation's worship services can become more outreaching.

Worship

Outreach Idea One:
Visitors' Day

The notion of inviting visitors to worship may have general appeal, but many of us have a hard time getting around to actually inviting someone. Designation of one Sunday a month, or even one per quarter, as visitors' day can serve to focus members' efforts on this important outreach opportunity.

Step One—Planning

A. The pastor will meet with the worship commission to do the following:
 1. Establish a schedule of visitors' days for the coming year.
 2. Develop a working understanding of the role of visitors' days in the life of the congregation.
    a. The purpose of visitors' days
    b. Specific characteristics desired and special needs to be met
    c. Planning procedures
    d. Evaluation procedures.
 3. Select individuals who will promote the program of visitors' days among the members.
 4. Clarify the worship commission's tasks.

B. Those responsible for promoting the program among the members have these tasks:
 1. Refine the working understanding of the program's role into a form that can be communicated to members in writing, in person, and by telephone.

2. Develop a plan for contacting all active members of the congregation.
   a. Share with them the purpose of visitors' days and the schedule of these days for the next six months.
   b. Obtain a commitment that they will invite at least one nonmember friend, relative, or neighbor to the first visitors' day.
3. Plan ways to remind members of each upcoming visitors' day and their commitment to invite someone to accompany them to worship. This can be accomplished through phone calls, personal reminders, bulletin announcements, and postcards.
4. Modify the above three steps into an ongoing plan of promotion for visitors' days.

C. Tasks for the worship commission
   1. Select a theme for each visitors' day that will be inclusive in its focus, free of RLDS jargon or exclusive references, and particularly relevant to life in the present.
   2. Discuss and adopt an approach to visitors' day services that will help visitors feel welcome, focus on common needs, and use scripture, testimony, and heritage in an affirmative way.
   3. Designate individuals or teams to plan the services for visitors' days with special attention to the following factors:
      a. Selection of hymns and scriptures that witness powerfully of Christ
      b. Opportunity through preaching or testimony for members to share a positive Christian witness

  c. Choice of persons to offer worship leadership who demonstrate competence, sincerity, and enthusiasm
4. Review the service outlines and personnel selections prepared by the planners and offer suggestions for improvement where appropriate.
5. Ensure that all arrangements are made so that the service will proceed as planned.

Step Two—Implementation

Conduct the worship services as planned on each visitors' Sunday.

Step Three—Evaluation

After each visitors' Sunday service hold an evaluation meeting including the pastor, members of the worship commission, and the persons responsible for promotion.

Step Four—Modification

Make changes in approach to and planning for subsequent visitors' Sundays based on suggestions emerging from the evaluation meeting.

Worship

Outreach Idea Two:
Community Worship Service

Developing a spirit of friendship and cooperation with other churches in the community can be an effective form of outreach. Although each denomination is different in important respects, they share some goals in common. Hosting a community worship service in celebration of a special season of the year can serve to express the common stewardship shared by all churches in a community. A service may be planned to celebrate Thanksgiving, Advent, Christmas, Holy Week, or some other occasion in which the spirit of cooperation between churches can be extended.

Step One—Planning

A. The pastor will do the following:
1. Meet with other congregational leaders to determine possible times of the year when a community worship service would be feasible.
2. Meet with other ministers in the community to assess the extent of their interest in supporting an interdenominational service.
3. In cooperation with representatives of other churches in the community, establish the date for the community service and clarify who will be responsible for various parts of the planning and preparation.

B. The worship commission will do the following:
1. Select a theme and focus for the service that

is seasonal, consistent with basic Christian (and Jewish if appropriate) understandings, and relevant to the lives of participants.
2. Appoint a team of persons (including members of other churches) to plan the service and select participants.
3. Make all necessary arrangements to ensure that the service will go according to plan.

C. Persons responsible for publicity and promotions will do the following:
1. Meet with representatives of other churches to plan for publicizing the service in each church and throughout the community. Media such as radio, television, and newspapers should be considered.
2. Obtain information about the proposed service from the worship commission and service-planning team.
3. Implement the plans for publicity.

Step Two—Implementation

Conduct the worship service on the planned date.

Step Three—Evaluation

A. Schedule an evaluation meeting including members of the worship commission, the service-planning team, persons responsible for publicity, and representatives of other churches.
B. Make tentative plans for future community worship services and establish a date to meet again to discuss specific strategies.

Worship

Outreach Idea Three: Outreach Testimonies

Congregational worship is an appropriate setting for members to share the good news of what they are doing to express their discipleship in the community. Enthusiastic personal testimonies shared by members who are involved in community ministries can motivate others to expand their outreach efforts. Inclusion of such testimonies on a regular basis in the congregation's worship can also contribute to a revitalization of the worship experience.

Step One—Planning
  A. The worship commission will decide the most effective way of including outreach testimonies in the congregation's worship services, giving attention to the following:
    1. Frequency of testimonies (how many times per month)
    2. Length of testimonies (how many minutes)
    3. Procedure for selecting and inviting people to share their testimonies.

  B. The worship commission will meet with members of the other commissions to discuss ways to identify members who are involved in outreach activities, and methods for selecting persons to testify.

  C. The worship commission will determine how best to inform the congregation of the plans to include outreach testimonies in worship services on a regular basis.

D. The worship commission will develop brief guidelines for use by worship planners, to include the following:
  1. Rationale for including outreach testimonies in worship
  2. A schedule of which services should or may include outreach testimonies
  3. Some examples of where outreach testimonies might be placed in order of service
     a. One testimony before or after a sermon
     b. Two or three testimonies as the principal avenues for sharing the word
     c. One testimony as a statement of commitment toward the end of the service
     d. One testimony as an offertory statement

E. Worship planners will include outreach testimonies in the services they plan where appropriate and invite individuals to share the testimonies. Participants should be given reasons why *they* are being asked to share, explanation of *what* they should focus their remarks on, and an estimate (in minutes) of the time allowed in the service for the testimony.

Step Two—Implementation

Hold the services as planned.

Step Three—Evaluation

The worship commission will meet with members of the other commissions and the pastor to discuss the effectiveness of the program after it has been going for several months and make necessary modifications for the future.

Worship

Outreach Idea Four: Visiting Speakers

Outreach is not a one-way venture. The church needs to invite the contributions of nonmembers as well as trying to meet their needs. By providing for persons in the community to offer ministry in our worship services on occasion, our worship is enriched, our contacts with individuals and organizations are expanded, and nonmembers come to view the church as interested in what goes on beyond its own walls and membership. The regular involvement of speakers from the community is an important expression of outreach.

Step One—Planning

A. The worship commission will discuss ways in which visiting speakers from the community can be involved in worship services, including preaching a sermon, sharing a testimony, and making an audiovisual presentation.

B. The worship commission will ask members of the congregation to help develop a list of potential speakers. This should include the topic on which the individual might speak, and name of member through whom contact might be made.

C. The worship commission will decide which services should or may include ministry by a visiting speaker.

D. The worship commission will communicate the desire to include visiting speakers to persons who are assigned to plan services.

E. Worship planners will provide opportunity for visiting speakers to share at appropriate places in the selected service.

F. Worship planners will select and contact visiting speakers, giving them reasons why *they* are being asked to share, explanation of *what* they should focus their remarks on, and an estimate (in minutes) of the time allowed in the service for the speaker.

Step Two—Implementation
Hold the services as planned.

Step Three—Evaluation
The worship commission will meet with other interested members of the congregation to evaluate the visiting speaker program after it has been going for several months and make necessary modifications for the future.

Worship

Outreach Idea Five:
Worship beyond the Church

We usually think of the congregation's worship as occurring in the church sanctuary or perhaps at a location elsewhere in the church building or at a campground. We often think of outreach as that which attracts people to the church building. An alternative view, however, can see the worship function of the church being taken beyond the sanctuary into the community. Some congregations provide weekly or monthly worship services in rest homes or other institutions where people live. On a smaller scale, some municipal governments invite ministers of various churches to offer prayer at the beginning of their meetings. Opportunities for the latter kind of ministry may be limited particularly in the United States where the issue of separation of church and state is sensitive. Congregations can, however, look for opportunities to reach out by taking worship to those community settings where it would be welcome.

Step One—Planning

    A. The pastor, worship commission, and Zionic relations commission will meet to consider where the congregation might provide worship opportunities including rest homes, hospitals, prisons, council meetings, and public events.

    B. The worship commission will make contact with the institutions which are seen to be the best possibilities for worship outreach. The purpose is to assess the interest of the institution, discuss possible approaches, determine the needs, and establish a schedule.

C. The worship commission will discuss the reports of those who have visited with institutional representatives and determine how the congregation can fill the needs. The following steps should be taken:
1. List the interested institutions and their specific needs.
2. Assess the congregation's resources (personnel and other) available for this program of ministry.
3. Prioritize the possible programs.
4. Select those which can be handled by the congregation.
5. Develop a specific proposal to take to the representatives of institutions which can be served.

D. The designated contact persons and members of the worship commission will work out the details of the program with representatives of the institutions.

Step Two—Implementation

The program of ministry will be conducted according to the agreement between the congregation and the institution.

Step Three—Evaluation

Members of the worship commission, and other individuals where appropriate, will meet with representatives of the institutions where ministry is being offered to evaluate the program and make changes affecting its continuation.

Outreach through Christian Education

By Janet and David Chobar

Christian education in the church school setting has often been overlooked as a vital tool for both religious growth and numerical expansion. Because of the missionary potential of every congregation's church school, Christian education can be viewed as an opportunity for outreach—an exciting opportunity to touch the lives of children and adults within your community.

God is helping the church grow and expand. The great Commission found in Matthew 28:19 (Inspired Version) is key to the Restoration movement. Christ commissions today's church to go into all the world "teaching them to observe all things whatsoever I have commanded you; and lo, I am with you always, unto the end of the world." This is challenging and encourages all who desire to assist the church school as it develops by "leaps and bounds."

There are many reasons to have hope for outreach through Christian education.

1. Christian education, at every congregational level, needs a shot in the arm. It needs more pushes from behind, better tender loving care, and greater enthusiasm. It has not yet reached a level of success that comes close to what it can be: an alive, vibrant, growing, outreaching ministry which enhances the congregation.
2. The church school has not been adequately understood and thus is not performing its essential responsibility. Most persons want and need clear

answers to the deep questions of life. A vital church school program provides important opportunities for exploration and dialogue.
3. The church school is a unique "bridge." It is one area of the church where all family members can participate and receive ministry at their own level of need.
4. Some studies indicate that there is a close relationship between initial patterns in church school enrollment and later patterns in church membership. One survey found that church school and church membership statistics were positively related. The study showed that church school enrollment was an accurate predictor of church membership figures five years later. Often it is not the fault of any existing program that is causing lack in numbers as much as it is the fault of a weak church school program four or five years ago!
5. Further studies reveal that parents often choose to attend a church for the sake of their children. Parents want their children to participate in a good church school program and many become interested in the church on that basis. A study by the Princeton Religious Research Center* published in 1978 inquired if parents wanted their children to receive religious instruction. A positive answer was given by 95 percent of the churched and 74 percent of the unchurched respondents. The "unchurched" are those who do not belong to *any* religious institution or who do not regularly attend any religious body. It is now estimated that 40 to 50 percent of the persons in every community are

---
*The Unchurched American, Princeton Research Center and the Gallup Organization, Inc., 1978.

unchurched. When asked to make a choice of the kind of religious instruction (Sunday school, parochial school, instruction at home, courses in public schools), the Sunday school (what we call "church school") received a 75 percent response from the churched and amazingly a 73 percent response from the unchurched. According to these statistics, "Sunday school" is still accepted by the general population as an important and effective agency of religious instruction.

6. Many of our congregations have seventy-five members or less. That is not unusual. United States national statistics show that of *all* Christian denominations meeting on a given Sunday, 50 percent have fifteen to seventy-five persons in attendance. Thus, most of the ideas which follow will be related to these smaller congregations. However, even the congregations having 250 or more attending members will be able to use some of these ideas and concepts.

God is our greatest source of help. Often it seems there are no solutions, but we discover God aiding us as we search. Through prayer, willingness to risk, and by expecting an answer to our questions when we have pushed to our own human limits, discoveries are made and adventures are experienced. God wants every person to be discovered and won to Christ.

- In what ways is my congregation's church school outreach-oriented?
- How have my thoughts concerning church school been more negative than positive? How can this be changed?
- If I want growth and expansion to occur in my

church school, where will my congregation begin?
- In what ways is my church school growing? Be specific.
- How do I know if my church school is expanding? List examples.
- Why do I believe that the church school can grow and expand?
- What are some changes that can come about in my congregation's church school? Which one should be improved first?
- In what ways am I willing to pay the price for seeing more children, youth, and adults taught a Christian way of discipleship?
- Do I really feel that "it sounds good but it'll never work!" If so, what questions must I have answered to change my mind?

Christian Education

Outreach Idea One:
Community Survey

Two major elements confront us in this outreach activity. First of all, what are people like in the community *immediately* within the vicinity of the church building? Are there many children, youth, or adults in the neighborhood who might consider attending your church? This survey enables you to find out what the immediate possibilities are within two or three blocks each direction from the church. If your congregation is rural, consider enlarging the area to all those homes within a one- to five-mile radius.

Secondly, the obvious concern which you are expressing is that *you are open for business!* Often, we do so little in the immediate area around the church. Consider this incident which took place in one of our congregations:

A lady tapped on the window of a church member's car as she walked by the church. The church member had just driven up to attend Sunday service. She said, "Excuse me, do you attend this church?" "Yes," replied the surprised member. "Do you want anybody from the neighborhood to come to church?" was the next question. "I have lived here eight years and no one has ever come to my home to invite me to attend your church!"

We must contact people at their door to let them know we are "in business." Over a period of time communities will become familiar with a church because of the consistent outreach efforts of its members.

Step One—Preliminary Planning

A. The Christian education commission members or the chairperson will obtain the following items:
   1. A large, detailed map of the city on which the community around the church can be located. Some of these maps are large enough to show each home lot on the streets adjacent to the church.
   2. Population information for the community. (See missionary outreach idea 2, "Charting a Course for Outreach," step 2.)

B. Invite persons to work in teams for a door-to-door canvass.
   1. Be specific about what you expect from each volunteer. People are looking for commitment during the '80s! They are most likely to commit themselves to a specific, well defined task.
   2. Organize the members into visiting teams.

C. Select date(s) to provide an hour or two of training for every team surveying the neighborhood.
   1. Open the training with prayer.
   2. Hand out copies of the survey form.
   3. Role-play visiting situations. Allow time for each team to role-play several times. It will make a great deal of difference in the actual visiting.

D. Set date(s) to conduct the survey.
   1. Consider "rain dates" in case of inclement weather.

2. Consider the neighborhood carefully. Pick an "ideal" weekend.
   a. Avoid holiday weekends or other times when people are likely to be gone.
   b. Remember—some people sleep late on Saturday.
   c. An ideal survey time may be during the week from 4:00 to 7:00 p.m. or from 7:00 to 9:00 p.m. Ask the Holy Spirit to guide you in your planning.

E. Develop your survey questionnaire. Remember two key items:
   1. The survey questionnaire must be short. You cannot ask persons ten detailed questions and expect to take fifteen to thirty minutes at their home. Assure them that you only need a minute or two of their time... and *mean it!*
   2. Design the questionnaire to obtain persons' *opinions.* Most persons welcome the opportunity to share their opinions on anything. Allow room for the address and any additional information you intend to collate or keep.

Model Survey Questionnaire

Do you REGULARLY attend a local church or synagogue? _____
  If yes,
What keeps you active?_____
_____

What kinds of Sunday school classes or Christian education classes do you or your children attend?

_____
_____

(If the respondent does not attend such classes, ask the next question.)
If you were looking for a church in the area, what kinds of things would you look for?

_____
_____

Do you have school-age children at home?
_____ Their ages? _____ (Assure them you are not asking for names, just ages)
What Bible study clases or subjects would you and your children attend if offered?

_____
_____

  Thank You!

   Address _____
   Name_____
   Surveyor _____

Step Two—The Outreach
- A. Meet at the church thirty minutes prior to beginning the survey.

- B. Share in prayer together. Prayer takes on special significance when you are about to venture out together, even for a survey.

- C. Give copies of the survey instrument to everyone. Do not pre-address the questionnaires. This enables the surveyors to record only the addresses of those who are actually contacted.

- D. Ask the surveyors to note the addresses of those persons not at home or who were not willing to answer any questions.
    1. You will find that only about 2 to 4 percent of those contacted will *not* be willing to give you their opinion.
    2. This survey is to gather opinions. If some neighbors do not want to give their opinion, do not be discouraged. Be as positive in your response as possible. You are a disciple representing the Reorganized Church of Jesus Christ of Latter Day Saints in your community.

- E. Decide a specific time to return to the church.

- F. Plan to go out to dinner, return to the church and have pizza or just have snacks and refreshments when you finish the survey activity.

- G. Discuss some of the positive responses and experiences of the day.

Step Three—Collate the materials by address and street. A computer is ideal for bringing this information together, especially the children's ages and proximity to the church.

Step Four—Follow-Up
   A. Chart or graph the ages of the youth in the homes you surveyed.
      1. Is there an abundance of a certain age group or spread?
      2. Was there a repetition of certain needs or interests which seemed to fit a pattern (for example, young married couples with pre-teen children, elderly with no children)?

   B. How do you intend to use this information for OUTREACH? As a commission, brainstorm the possibilities indicated by the survey.

   C. As a commission, use this information to begin meeting needs in the immediate community. Do not be concerned if neighbors do not attend church or are not interested in baptism.

   D. Organize a class and begin advertising its offering to those homes who were interested in the specific subject.

   E. Develop a creative brochure which has photographs of each one of your church school teachers and what subjects their classes will be studying the coming semester.
      1. Distribute the brochures to the entire neighborhood.

2. Keep publicity in front of the people. Remember, we are letting them know that we are "in business for Christ."
3. Consider mailing one or all of these new tracts:
   - A Church That Values Children
   - A Christ-Centered Church
   - A Church That Affirms and Upholds Family Life
   - A Church Based on the Bible
   - A Church Involved in Community
   - A Church That Invites You to Share

Christian Education

Outreach Idea Two:
Training for Outreach

The book *Growth: A New Vision for the Sunday School* can serve as a tool to motivate members toward a new vision of programming with outreach as a focus rather than maintenance.

A. In preparing for the curriculum of the church school, include an eight-week class for church leaders using the resource *Growth: A New Vision for the Sunday School* by Charles Arn, Donald McGavran, and Win Arn. A companion kit is available through the Christian Education Commission or Missionary Office for an eight-hour workshop.
   1. Invite potential and current teachers or those involved in leadership of programs such as youth leadership, women's groups, and singles.
   2. Order books from Herald House for class use.
   3. Arrange for a teacher and share your hopes for what the class is to accomplish.
   4. Arrange the classroom space to allow the group to meet in a circle.
   5. Encourage action assignments to put into practice one idea from each of the weekly sessions.

B. Optional: Use the book in a series of training workshops for those presently involved in teaching in the church school.

Christian Education

Outreach Idea Three:
Monthly Fun Activity Night

If you will investigate your town, city, or neighborhood, you will likely make contact with officials who are willing to talk to you about needs in your local community. In this time of declining federal funding of various projects, numerous small groups need help.

In one town, the congregation found that no one was providing activities for mentally retarded adults between the ages of eighteen and thirty. This was not an easy group to consider. Every town or community has someone who has been overlooked in funding, caring, or concern. It was discovered that the parents of these eighteen- to thirty-year-old mentally retarded adults were extremely concerned because no one was ministering to this special group—there were no unique Christian education opportunities available.

The Christian education commission began developing a fun night once a quarter, which eventually was held once a month. Beginning with fun social activities these families soon became familiar with the building and many of the members. The eventual goal is to offer church school opportunities especially geared for retarded adults. Qualified personnel who have special education training and congregationally supported training for members interested in teaching this special group will be provided. The five-year goal is to minister to retarded adults and their parents in a special Christian education mission.

What special needs exist in your community? What unique opportunities are there to reach out in specialized Christian education ministry?

Step One—Preliminary Planning
   A. The Christian education commission will consider the special needs of a "target group" to whom the congregation can minister.

   B. Meet with a representative or spokesperson for this group.
      1. Social worker
      2. Member of the department of social services
      3. Town committeeperson
      4. Nursing home recreation director

   C. Ask what the needs are.
      1. Decide what are potential fun activities. Make a list:
         a. Professional/semi-pro sports activities (baseball, football, hockey, tennis)
         b. Movie night (you can rent your own.)
         c. Roller skating, bowling
         d. Museums
         e. Special schools
      2. Consider personal safety. If all persons are in wheelchairs, make sure the church and other locations have access ramps and other necessary equipment and facilities.

Step Two—Scheduling a Meeting
   A. Decide if there is enough interest to continue the project. Do not begin unless you are willing to consider a two- to five-year commitment.

More harm is done by beginning and not following through, than by not beginning at all.

B. Locate resources, such as Christian movie rental agencies. Many of them have one-day service for mailing excellent 16mm films or videocassettes. Obtain a copy of *Resource Directory* from the Resource Center in the Auditorium for current films, videotapes, and film strips.

C. Ask for church discounts. Tell merchants about the groups you are ministering to and your goals.

D. Use maximum publicity.
   1. Plan far enough in advance to allow time to develop attractive announcements.
   2. Flood the community with the information.
   3. Utilize community bulletin boards. Plan to have the activity at the church. It is important to let the community know that you care for people.

Step Three—The Outreach

A. Never cancel an activity due to lack of numbers. Quality is more important than quantity. It is hoped that attendance will increase.

B. Provide transportation to and from each activity.

Step Four—Long-Range Christian Education Goals

As the monthly activity nights progress, the commission along with representatives of the special group will meet to consider Christian education opportunities which can be offered.

A. Sunday or weekday Bible study classes

B. Special interest courses such as communication, relationship, ethics/values.

Step Five—Follow-up
A. Use a telephone chain or letter-reply card system to obtain feedback from the group.
  1. How can the monthly activities be improved?
  2. What new resources, film rental agencies, equipment, facilities could be utilized?

B. Do not be concerned with converting people. The intent of this project is to minister to persons who are not being ministered to by anyone else.

C. Consider home visitations to get to know persons in the special group in more personal and caring ways.

D. Be a witness of the gospel and how the gospel impacts persons at home, at work, and in all aspects of life.

E. Conduct ongoing training for those leading the program.

F. Constantly look at your facilities. How can they be made safer or improved to better serve the needs being observed?

G. Obtain all the feedback you can, the more the better.

H. Begin architectural planning for a new Christian education wing adjacent to your sanctuary because you are going to need it!

Christian Education

Outreach Idea Four:
Vacation Church School Ice Cream Social

Most churches put out a large sign to advertise vacation church school (or vacation Bible school). Next year do something so spectacular that everyone will be talking about it for years to come.

One month prior to your vacation church school, distribute leaflets to your neighborhood near the church with the following advertisement:

FREE ICE CREAM!

Free Ice Cream

The bearer of this coupon is entitled to one bowl of free ice cream per family member at the _____ church.

Free Ice Cream

NEVER LET IT BE SAID
YOU GET ONLY WHAT YOU
PAY FOR!

We want to introduce you and your children to our neighborhood church at _____. There are no gimmicks. We invite your children to attend our vacation Bible school, a week of fun, learning, and exploring. Come and enjoy a free bowl of ice cream—we want to meet you and tell you about our exciting VCS coming up next month!

VACATION CHURCH SCHOOL IS FUN!

Dates: month, days, year

Step One—Preliminary Planning

A. Plan your vacation church school (VCS) six to eight months in advance.

B. Obtain VCS material from Herald House and begin determining personnel and resources.

C. Plan to hold the ice cream social at least two weeks prior to the date of the VCS.

D. Contact local ice cream companies or restaurants. Many ice cream shops only require that you tell them how many people you expect and they provide the paper goods, toppings, nuts, vanilla/chocolate ice cream, whipped cream, and even the scoops. In return, put up huge signs indicating who donated the ice cream or provided it at a discounted rate.

E. Recruit persons as scoopers, toppers, dippers, or whatever you need to provide a smorgasboard ice cream line—much like a potluck. *Invite parents from the community to help.*

Step Two—The Social

A. Display the VCS theme and material. The puppets and puppet stage will draw great attention.

B. Provide a top-notch fifteen- to thirty-minute introduction of the theme of the VCS, Bible principles to be taught, and the crafts and fun you will have during the week. Introduce the teachers and special helpers.

C. Have some children from the neighborhood participate in a small puppet show during the introduction mentioned above.

D. Pre-register as many children as possible.

E. Invite all persons to sign a guest book.

Step Three—Follow-up
A. Develop a telephone campaign to contact *all* who come to the ice cream social *one or two weeks* prior to the actual VCS.

B. Write a letter or card to *each* home which is represented at the ice cream social.

C. Add the names of those who attend the ice cream social to selected congregational newsletters or mailings sent out monthly or quarterly.

D. Ask any mothers or fathers who seem particularly interested to help with the VCS.

E. Put the actual cost for this ice cream social in next year's missionary or evangelism budget.

F. Make this an annual event.

G. Do not be discouraged if only a dozen or so people come the first year. Word will get around for next year's event.

H. Remember, you are serving ice cream to neighbors. This is not an ice cream social for the church. All church members will be active in the serving line or be specially oriented to make every single person who comes to the ice cream social feel welcome, wanted, and needed.

Pastoral Care Outreach
By Charles Mader

Historically, members of the church have viewed pastoral care as a ministry focused on persons within the fellowship. When the goal is to win new members, ministry to persons outside the fellowship has generally been labeled community service or evangelism. For practical as well as philosophical reasons church leaders have separated pastoring and evangelizing. Members and ministers have seen these two activities as unrelated in the program sense. But pastoring and evangelizing can be viewed as a common or unified activity. This may require some reframing of terms. Developing this "new view" is the primary goal of this chapter.

As you read further it is recommended that you put on your "mystical hat" rather than your "scientific hat." You are invited to think of the church in its universal sense rather than its organizational sense. You are encouraged to look past the walls, lines, and partitions that artificially, but sometimes necessarily, separate persons into groups. Release yourself, for a few moments, from the normal human tendency to think about persons as insiders and outsiders, as good and bad, as ill and well, as saved and unsaved, as God's people and Gentiles.

Pastoral evangelism is the act of meeting God at another person's point of need, pain, brokenness, and separation from God and from other persons. It is a unique form of healing ministry that does not shrink from suffering or run from another person's pain. This ministry differs from traditional concepts of Christian service. The goal of this ministry is to be "present" to another person's need and suffering rather than attempting to eliminate the pain or the problem.

Pastoral ministry focuses on the person and the person's spiritual journey. This is not an attempt to avoid the problems and needs, but the pastoral evangelist recognizes that some problems cannot be solved, some loss cannot be returned, and some pain cannot be avoided. However, all suffering can be attended to by pastoral ministry.

Pastoral evangelism involves a partnership with God. It is a choice to be where God is. God can always be found at the point where creation is suffering. To be pastoral evangelists we are admonished to visit the sick, attend to the needs of the poor, and comfort those who mourn or are alone.

An example of pastoral evangelism is the Community Assistance Services, a Division of the Independence Sanitarium and Hospital. This division of the San provides pastoral services to the surrounding community. These services are offered to persons of many denominations. The staff and volunteers who provide a variety of services are trained to be pastoral evangelists. The following definition of pastoring has been developed as a guide for these services:

Definition of Pastoring

Our concept of pastoring is designed to affirm the wholeness of personhood in every life-changing experience.

Pastoring is caring for persons in ways that affirm them as worthwhile and able to preside over their own lives.

The opposite of pastoring is to relate to persons as if they are victims who must be managed and controlled. Illness, crisis, and moments of significant loss are times when individuals are tempted to feel and behave like victims. This negation of self is often the overwhelming self-image when one has a life-threatening disease and when one faces any point of life change.

Pastoral services focus on healing, whether or not curing is possible. Traditional medical services, social services, and many religious programs have been designed to fix, eliminate, rehabilitate, and cure.

Pastoral services, as we envision them, are designed to connect with persons at the point of their suffering and to help them adjust to losses which are part of every facet of human life. Pastoring is serving in ways that affirm and develop strengths and enhance individuals' ability to be in charge of their own lives.

Pastoral services include visiting, counseling, educational programs, hands-on helping activities, and organizational interventions which facilitate pastoring behavior in persons, families, groups, and the community.

—Adapted from
   Independence Sanitarium and Hospital
   Community Assistance Services
   October 1983

High pressure forms of evangelism can be unhelpful and even abusive to persons in personal crisis. Everyone needs someone who will not run from suffering but who will be a pastor to the pain of living.

Pastoral evangelism involves opening our eyes and ears to the life struggle of those who are already part of our life space. We do not begin by changing careers or getting a new academic degree. In this regard we are reminded of the words of the prophet Jeremiah to the Israelites who had been carried off to Babylon by King Nebuchadnezzar: "Seek the peace of the city whither I have caused you to be carried away captives, and pray unto the Lord for it; for in the peace thereof shall ye have peace" (Jeremiah 29:7).

Techniques for Pastoral Evangelism

The techniques or skills of pastoral evangelism enable personal freedom. Pastoral evangelism helps persons discover their kingdom-building potentials. This form of ministry grows out of the following basic assumptions about people and the human condition in relationship to God.
1. God is already at work in every person's life.
2. Bad things do happen to good people.
3. Healing and curing are not the same thing and do not always happen together.
4. Righteousness is not a precondition to a relationship with God but is the intended result of the relationship.
5. Emotional pain is a normal part of our spiritual journey and cannot be avoided nor eliminated from human experience.
6. God promises that we will be attended in our

suffering, not that we will be spared the suffering of human life.
7. Well-meaning people injure those they care about, sometimes even in an attempt to be helpful or to give ministry.
8. Pain, problems, and confusion are not always the result of personal acts of sin.
9. Losses and grief are normal aspects of the human spiritual journey.
10. Healing ministry seeks to protect a person's rights. It enhances persons' ability to exercise agency in their own lives regardless of the circumstances that exist at the moment.

Becoming a pastoral evangelist requires ongoing preparation. It begins with a valid, intimate, personal relationship with Jesus Christ. This relationship is supported by study of scripture and of all good books. This relationship also involves a prayer life that is rich in individual and corporate experience.

Central to the personal-spiritual preparation for pastoral evangelism is the awareness that suffering is a natural part of human life. Pastoral evangelists must be in touch with their own pain and suffering in order to be present to that experience in others.

Pastoral Care

Outreach Idea One:
Orientation to Pastoral Evangelism

The exciting possibilities of pastoral evangelism can be explored by your congregation and community. Many of the residents in your neighborhood may have been personally touched by loss and other crises. It is possible that these persons will be interested in some of the issues outlined in the introduction such as dealing with grief, pain, problems, and confusion. Plan a series of meetings, a weekend seminar, or regular adult classes. Publicize the event throughout your community. Utilize a skilled discussion facilitator to discuss the list of assumptions mentioned in this chapter. Explore some of the traditional assumptions of pastoral caring. Discuss new possibilities of pastoral ministry in the community. Brainstorm the kinds of changes that will need to be made and the kind of growth that will occur as pastoral outreach gains momentum.

Step One—Initial Planning

The pastoral care commissioner and commission members will meet with the pastor to do these things:

A. Determine the need for community orientation to pastoral outreach.

B. State the desired outcome.

C. Develop a project proposal stating dates and goals.

D. Write job descriptions and suggest persons who can serve on the project.

E. Consider other community agencies which could be invited to share.

Step Two: Getting Started
A. Duties of the project coordinator
   1. Recruit persons to fill project responsibilities.
   2. Contact community resource persons.
   3. Coordinate the planning and implementation of the project and hold periodic meetings with all persons involved to coordinate efforts.
   4. Submit a tentative budget to the pastoral care commissioner and pastor for approval.

B. Duties of the publicity and promotion coordinator
   1. Recruit volunteers.
   2. Arrange for posters, bulletin inserts, and flyers.
   3. Prepare newspaper and radio advertisements.
   4. Coordinate community mailings and canvassing.
   5. Submit a budget to the project coordinator for approval.

C. Duties of the facilities and physical arrangements coordinator
   1. Recruit volunteers.
   2. Arrange seating.

    3. Arrange for parking and audiovisual and sound equipment.
    4. Arrange for clean-up.
    5. Submit a budget to the project coordinator for approval.

D. Duties of the refreshments coordinator
    1. Recruit volunteers.
    2. Provide refreshments.
    3. Provide utensils and serving arrangements.
    4. Arrange for clean-up.
    5. Submit a budget to the project coordinator for approval.

E. Duties of the hospitality coordinator
    1. Recruit a team of volunteers.
    2. Greet every participant.
    3. Fill out personal data cards on each participant (name, phone number, address, active church affiliation).
    4. Distribute name tags.
    5. Coordinate registration.
    6. Give all participant information to the outreach coordinator for follow-up.
    7. Submit a budget to the project coordinator for approval.

Step Three—Holding the Event

The project coordinator will do the following:

A. Host the activity.

B. Ensure a smooth-flowing and flexible schedule.

C. Provide support and assistance to the guest resource persons.

D. Coordinate the efforts of all project personnel.

Step Four—Follow-up
  A. The project coordinator will do the following:
   1. Review the responsibilities with the project staff to see that all tasks are completed.
   2. Give special support to the outreach/follow-up team.
   3. Receive and finalize expense reports to submit to the pastor or bishop's agent.

  B. Evaluation of the project will be carried out by the pastor, pastoral care commissioner, and pastoral care commission.

Pastoral Care
Outreach Idea Two:
Loss and Grief Workshop

Persons who are experiencing grief because of a significant loss can find help and healing. Invite local professionals to conduct a series of classes or a weekend workshop on death and dying and on grief related to other life experiences involving losses. It is important in this activity to focus on grief as being normal, although painful. As the activity progresses your congregation may want to consider sponsoring and organizing grief support groups for the community. These support groups would meet once or twice a week indefinitely.

Step One—Initial Planning

The pastoral care commissioner and commission members will meet with the pastor to do the following:

A. Determine the need for a loss and grief workshop.

B. State the desired outcome.

C. Develop a project proposal stating dates and goals.

D. Brainstorm tasks which will need to be accomplished and suggest persons who can serve on the project.

E. Consider local professionals and agencies who could conduct the series of classes or workshop.

Pastoral Care

Outreach Idea Three: Community Course on Forgiveness

Throughout the development of any relationship, disagreement will arise from time-to-time concerning lifestyles, opinions, expectations, and personal desires. Because all of us are unique creations of God, these differences and perceptions are a natural part of any relationship and a necessary ingredient in the growth and maturing process of persons. An indispensable facet of interpersonal relationships is the active concept of "forgiveness." Cultivating the skills and spirit of forgiveness will allow persons to move through conflict in creative and positive ways. It will bring increase to situations which would otherwise falter and become mired in devastated feelings and crushed self-images. Organize a weekend or weekday class for adults using the book *Forgive and Forget* by Lewis Smedes. Publicize the series of classes through bulletin inserts and community flyers. Make sure the class is available at a time which is convenient for community residents as well as church members. Advertise the activity as one which would relate to couples, singles, and young persons.

Step One—Initial Planning

The pastoral care commissioner and commission members will meet with the pastor to do the following:

    A. Determine the need for a community course on forgiveness.

B. State the desired outcome.

C. Develop a project proposal stating dates and goals.

D. Write job descriptions and suggest persons who can serve on the project.

E. Brainstorm a list of professionals, congregational members, or community leaders from which an instructor for the class can be chosen.

Follow steps two through four in "Outreach Idea One" to complete the activity.

Pastoral Care
Outreach Idea Four:
Human Communication Skills Workshop

Enlist trained church members or community professionals to provide several classes designed to improve interpersonal communication skills. This program will emphasize self-awareness, verbal and nonverbal communication, and a heavy emphasis on developing the skills of listening to goals, values, feelings, and the needs of others. Publicize this activity throughout your community. Publicize the event as one which would be valuable for parents and their children, married couples, and singles.

Step One—Intitial Planning

The pastoral care commissioner and commission members will meet with the pastor to do the following:

A. Determine the need for a communication skills workshop.

B. State the desired outcome.

C. Develop a project proposal stating dates and goals.

D. Write job descriptions and suggest persons who can serve on the project.

E. Consider a list of trained church members or community professionals qualified to teach the classes.

Follow steps two through four in "Outreach Idea One" to complete the activity.

Pastoral Care

Outreach Idea Five:
God and I Communion Skills

Promote a series of classes or a special workshop designed to deepen relationships with God. Advertise this event as a community service project. All persons will benefit by an intensive program aimed at expanding the human perspective of our relationship with the Creator. Topics might include these:
1. Scripture study focusing on God's historical and present-day efforts to reach out to communicate with persons
2. Keeping a personal spiritual journal
3. Meditation skills and techniques
4. Prayer as interpersonal communication

Step One—Initial Planning

The pastoral care commissioner and commission members will meet with the pastor to do the following:
- A. Determine the need for a series of classes designed to deepen relationships with God.
- B. State the desired outcome.
- C. Develop a project proposal stating dates and goals.
- D. Write job descriptions and suggest persons who can serve on the project.
- E. Consider a list of persons qualified to teach the different topics suggested in the introduction to this outreach idea.

Follow steps two through four in "Outreach Idea One" to complete the activity.

Pastoral Evangelism
Recommended Reading List

Boyer, Ernest, Jr. *A Way in the World: Family Life As a Spiritual Discipline.* New York: Harper & Row, 1984.

Caulfield, Sean. *The Experience of Praying.* Ramsey, New Jersey: Paulist Press, 1980.

Claypool, John. *Tracks of a Fellow Struggler.* Waco, Texas: Word Books, 1976.

Dyckman, Katherine Marie, and L. Patrick Carrol. *Inviting the Mystic, Supporting the Prophet: An Introduction to Spiritual Direction.* Ramsey, New Jersey: Paulist Press, 1981.

Foster, Richard J. *The Celebration of Discipline: The Path to Spiritual Growth.* New York: Harper & Row, 1978.

Kubler-Ross, Elisabeth, and Mal Warshaw. *To Live Until We Say Good-Bye.* Englewood-Cliffs, New Jersey: Prentice-Hall, Inc., 1978.

Kushner, Harold S. *When Bad Things Happen to Good People.* New York: Schocken Books, 1981.

Lewis, C. S. *A Grief Observed.* New York: Bantam Books, 1976.

Marty, Martin E. *A Cry of Absence: Reflections for the Winter of the Heart.* New York: Harper & Row, 1983.

McNeill, Morrison, and Henri J. M. Nouwen. *Compassion: A Reflection on the Christian Life.* Garden City, New York: Doubleday & Company, Inc., 1982.

Miller, William A. *Make Friends with Your Shadow: How to Accept and Use Positively the Negative Side of Your Personality.* Minneapolis: Augsburg Publishing House, 1981.

Moustakas, Clark E. *Loneliness.* Englewood-Cliffs, New Jersey: Prentice-Hall, Inc., 1961.

Nouwen, Henri J. M. *A Cry for Mercy: Prayers from The Genesee.* Garden City, New York: Doubleday & Company, Inc., 1981.

──────. *The Way of the Heart: Desert Spirituality and Contemporary Ministry.* New York: Seabury Press, Inc., 1981.

──────. *The Wounded Healer: Ministry in Contemporary Society.* Garden City, New York: Doubleday & Company, Inc., 1979.

Peck, M. Scott. *The Road Less Traveled: A New Psychology of Love, Traditional Values and Spiritual Growth.* New York: Simon & Schuster, 1978.

Smedes, Lewis B. *Forgive & Forget: Healing the Hurts We Don't Deserve.* New York: Harper & Row, 1984.

Soelle, Dorothee. *Suffering.* Translated by Everett R. Kalin. Philadelphia: Fortress Press, 1975.

Tournier, Paul. *Creative Suffering.* New York: Harper & Row, 1983.

──────. *Fatigue in Modern Society.* Atlanta: John Knox Press, 1965.

──────. *The Gift of Feeling.* Atlanta: John Knox Press, 1981.

Worden, J. William. *Grief Counseling and Grief Therapy: A Handbook for the Mental Health Practitioner.* New York: Springer Publishing Company, 1982.

Yankelovich, Daniel. *New Rules: Searching for Self-Fulfillment in a World Turned Upside Down.* New York: Random Houise, 1981.

Stewardship Outreach

By Lee Cummins

Stewardship is the response of my people to the ministry of my Son.
—Doctrine and Covenants 147:5a

This scripture comes to mind frequently as we attempt to understand the message of love that is at the very center of Christ's ministry. Slowly our eyes and hearts open to see and feel the genuine love of God. This love is a redemptive, self-replenishing presence which fills and enlarges our lives and brings healing. Our response to this love is our stewardship. It is also self-replenishing. As we give our love freely in response to Christ's ministry, we experience a filling and enlarging of our lives.

This is so within the stewardship of our church family. Whenever our church fellowship extends itself in genuine love and caring to neighbors, individuals, or the wider community, there occurs vibrant expansion of the church. This "other-centered" nurturing love is our stewardship and is "required alike of all those who seek to build the kingdom" (Doctrine and Covenants 147:5a). We are accountable to extend our stewardship of caring to all who stand in need of Christ's ministry. In giving, we are filled. Without giving and caring there is emptiness and alienation.

An inmate of Sing Sing prison in New York wrote in a poem titled "Search for Love":

> To search for love is futile in this den
> Of sad, but deadly men, whose limp ardor
> Drifts in this prison sea, seeking warm harbors.
> by Henry Johnson. *The Light from Another Country: Poetry*

from *American Prisons*. Greenfield Center, New York: Greenfield Review Press.

He goes on to describe this futile search for love in the midst of shame and death and lonely prison cells. Even though the search is, in his words, hopeless, it *must* continue, for, "there's far too much at stake: To live unloved makes us cold, cruel, remote."

This poem expresses an extreme situation and yet it requires only casual observation for us to become aware of the heartache and pain of those around us—those who feel empty, alone, and alienated. Alcoholism, drug abuse, violence, immorality, and suicide are just a few of the symptoms displayed daily by persons who feel this void and sense of separation. The search for love continues. It is *here* that we must live out our stewardship of caring.

Jesus offered warmth for coldness, tenderness for cruelty, gatheredness and trust to replace the chilling remoteness experienced by the unloved. He came to minister to and free the captive, whether behind a prison wall or bound in a thousand other ways that are not seen by the eye but felt by the soul. We reach out and offer ministry in his name. We choose to be accountable in the midst of those who choose irresponsibility. Our stewardship is revealed as we come together in mutual support. Through the self-replenishing activity of our caring, we have the strength and desire to reach out to the alienated and unloved persons around us.

The need to share our stewardship of love is evident in every community where the church has a presence. Our caring takes many forms: neighborhood financial planning seminars, environmental and recycling efforts, and community stewardship projects. No matter what form our caring takes, it is essential that the life-changing love of Christ permeate life's circumstance and offer healing and wholeness where darkness and brokenness have taken root. This is our response to the ministry of Christ: to be outreaching in our stewardship, to be accountable for our caring, and to touch the lives of others with the love and reconciliation of Christ.

Stewardship

Outreach Idea One:
Bridging the Connection Gap

By Lee Cummins

When persons in a neighborhood have family problems and need help they often do not know where to turn. This is especially true for those who do not have a church or support group of their own. It is also true for persons who are reluctant to confess to their pastors the sensitive nature of personal or family discord. All around us people are asking for help and support in coping with a variety of social ills. This is an opportunity for the church to take seriously its stewardship in the community.

The church can be a bridge to help those in need to "connect" (that is, to get hooked up) with the public agencies and community services which can best respond to particular concerns. The telephone book is not enough. The church can help to bridge the "connection gap."

As part of the stewardship effort for your church, sponsor a "bridge connecting" event. Invite neighbors, friends, and church members to a special program to get acquainted with representatives of local public or private human service agencies. These representatives can explain the nature of services offered, the cost of services, and how the public can connect with the right service for their need. Plan for the pastor to share the ministries offered by your church. Provide refreshments and time for visiting. Be sure that all visitors are welcomed and have follow-up ministry prepared.

Step One—Initial Planning and Organization
A. The pastor will meet with the stewardship commission five months prior to the event.
   1. Decide on the agencies and resource persons to be represented.
      a. In a city or large urban area it may be necessary to focus on only a few of the many services and persons available.
      b. Review the make-up of the neighborhood around the church. Are there a great number of young families, senior citizens, blue collar workers, or ethnic groups?
      c. Consider the regional and local factors. Is there a high incidence of unemployment, rape, marital discord, or suicide among youth?
      d. In light of the people who may attend the event, what services could most appropriately match their concerns?
   2. Decide on the target audience.
      a. Neighbors around the church
      b. Unchurched friends and relatives of church members
      c. Members
      d. The community at large.
   3. Select and recruit the project coordinator who will do the following:
      a. Assist in the planning of the event.
      b. Assist in the selection and recruiting of other key persons.
      c. Facilitate the coordination of the activities needed to prepare for and carry out the event.

d. Report progress to the stewardship commission and the pastor.
   e. Review and act on budgetary matters.
   f. Carry out an evaluation after the event.
4. Finalize the date.
5. List the primary and secondary human service agencies and persons to be contacted.
   a. Primary services are those agencies to be represented.
   b. Secondary services are those agencies for which information and literature will be made available.

B. The project coordinator will meet with the stewardship commission and pastor to do these things:
   1. Develop a time line for the tasks to be completed.
   2. Determine the funds available to support the project and establish a budget.
   3. Develop a list of persons needed to carry out the various tasks (publicity, hospitality, agency liaison, outreach ministry, refreshments, facility).

Step Two—Putting It Together

A. The project coordinator and stewardship commission members will begin recruiting key leaders for the following responsibilities:
   1. The agency liaison
      a. Recruit two additional volunteers
      b. Contact primary agencies to visit personally, and select three or four agencies willing to send a representative to make a brief presentation;

    c. Request information and literature from primary and secondary agencies.
    d. Send a letter to all agencies visited or those responding to requests for information thanking them for their time.
    e. Send a letter to those agencies who are sending a representative thanking them in advance and confirming the time and place and expectations and including directions to the church.
    f. Telephone participating agencies a week in advance to obtain the name of their representative, if not previously settled, and make arrangements for audiovisual equipment needed.
    g. Arrange to introduce each speaker at the event.
    h. Send out thank-you notes to each agency and representative after the event.
2. The publicity coordinator
    a. Recruit volunteers.
    b. Arrange for posters to be made and placed in various community locations.
    c. Prepare advertisements and contact newspapers and radio stations.
    d. Prepare flyers for mass mailing and neighborhood canvassing.
    e. Keep the membership aware of upcoming events through bulletin announcements.
    f. Develop a budget.
3. The refreshment coordinator
    a. Recruit help.
    b. Secure sufficient supplies.
    c. Prepare refreshments and make arrangements for serving.

       d. Arrange for clean-up.
       e. Develop a budget.
4. The hospitality coordinator
       a. Recruit members to welcome all visitors.
       b. Select two or three people to have visitors fill out visitor information cards.
5. The facility coordinator
       a. Recruit help.
       b. Arrange seating.
       c. Provide parking-directional signs or parking attendants if needed.
       d. Arrange for microphones and audio-visual setup.
       e. Provide display tables for community services literature and church literature (particularly pastoral care pamphlet series).
       f. Arrange for clean-up.
6. The outreach coordinator
       a. Recruit volunteers for home visits after the event. Visits should communicate a positive "we care" attitude.
       b. Carry out the visits to all non-church friends who attended the event.
          (1) Share a brochure* which describes services offered.
          (2) Give a "Care Bear" button, "The Good Shepherd Wants Ewe" button, or something similar to children.
          (3) Invite the people you are visiting to come to church.

---

*The brochure should provide basic information about the human service agencies in the local community. If material of this sort is already available, use it. It would be well to have this information available along with a brochure describing your local church and the services which your church provides.

      c. Write a note of thanks to all visitors who attended the program (if they have already been visited, express appreciation for their having you in their home).
      d. Submit a budget to the project coordinator.
  B. The project coordinator will meet with coordinators.
    1. Review responsibilities.
    2. Review time lines for the accomplishment of each responsibility.
    3. Review the budget requests and arrive at a total budget for the project.

Step Three—Holding the Event

The agency liaison coordinator will moderate the program.
  A. Keep questions and answers moving forward.
  B. Ensure a flexible time frame for speakers.
  C. Close the program with remarks by the pastor.

Step Four—Follow-up

The project coordinator will do the following:
  A. Review responsibilities with the coordinators to see that all tasks are completed.
    1. Give special support to the home visiting following the event.
    2. Receive final expense reports and submit a written report to the pastor.

  B. Evaluation will be carried out by the pastor, stewardship commission, and coordinators.

Stewardship Outreach

Outreach Idea Two:
Financial Planning for Singles

Plan an all-day workshop or a series of classes dealing with the financial concerns of single persons. Enlist help from the congregation as well as representatives from the community such as banks, insurance companies, social security offices, and law firms.

Publicize the event in the local newspaper and with letters to various churches in the community. Make sure members of the congregation are aware of the event and encourage them to bring unchurched friends and relatives.

Step One—Preliminary Planning

A. Six months before the event the stewardship commission will meet.
   1. Determine a time line for the event.
   2. Decide where the event will take place.
   3. Define the audience as persons who have never married or are divorced or widowed.
   4. Develop a survey form to interview the participants and to determine their needs and concerns related to financial planning.
   5. Form survey teams to acquire the information.
   6. Schedule a meeting in one month to report survey results.

B. Five months before the event the stewardship commission will meet.
   1. Determine a program based on the survey information.

2. Set goals.
3. Develop the following list of persons to organize and implement the various tasks involved to make the program meaningful:
    a. The program coordinator
        (1) Recruits volunteers to help on the program committee.
        (2) Develops the program schedule and format.
        (3) Checks with community resource persons (insurance agents, bankers, or financial planners), World Church personnel, and local individuals to staff the program and secure their commitment.
        (4) Develops an evaluation form for use at the end of the workshop.
        (5) Develops a budget for the stewardship commission's approval.
    b. The publicity and promotion coordinator
        (1) Recruits volunteers to work as a publicity and promotion committee.
        (2) Determines time lines for publicizing the event.
        (3) Prints fliers and other materials for promotion.
        (4) Secures newspaper ads, bulletin announcements, or radio spots.
        (5) Develops a budget to submit to the stewardship commission for approval.
    c. The facilities coordinator
        (1) Recruits volunteers for the facilities committee.
        (2) Secures needed audiovisual equipment.

(3) Makes sure the public address system is set up.
(4) Arranges for classroom space and preparation.
(5) Arranges for all necessary supplies.
(6) Purchases necessary items for a health break.
(7) Arranges for seating, registration table, and name tags.

C. Once the coordinators have been chosen, the stewardship commission will meet with them to clarify tasks and finalize the date of the workshop. Set bi-weekly meeting dates to coordinate the preparation. Make sure all persons know that the purpose of the event is to help singles of the congregation and community with their current financial concerns.

Step Two—Planning Meetings

Hold bi-weekly meetings to coordinate efforts until activity date.

Step Three—Implementation

Hold the workshop.

Step Four—Evaluation

Hold a meeting of the committee to evaluate the workshop.

Step Five—Follow-up

Have teams available to do follow up with notes and visits to unchurched participants.

Step Six—Follow-up Workshop
Make plans for a follow-up workshop based on the evaluations.

Stewardship

Outreach Idea Three:
Emphasizing Wills Seminar
By Claude Rains, Jr.

Plan a five-hour "wills emphasis" program. Invite community experts to conduct the seminar (lawyers, judges, bankers, or estate planners).

Publicize the event in the local newspaper. Make sure members of the congregation are aware of the event and encourage them to bring friends, relatives, and others they know.

Step One—Preliminary Planning

A. Four months before the event the stewardship commission will meet.
   1. Set a date and time for the seminar.
   2. Determine where the event will be held.
   3. Determine the target audience (young, middle, or senior adults).
   4. Discuss the subjects to be included in the seminar and set goals.
   5. Schedule a second meeting in two weeks to finalize plans.

B. The stewardship commission will meet to assign various tasks to be done.
   1. The program coordinator
      a. Develop the program schedule and format.
      b. Secure community resource persons to lead the various class sessions (World Church, district, and regional personnel can be used to staff the program).
      c. Develop an evaluation form for use at the conclusion of the seminar.

       d. Secure any audiovisuals needed for the event.
   2. The publicity and promotion coordinator
       a. Make a time line and plan of action for publicizing the event.
       b. Print materials to publicize the event and place newspaper ads and radio spots.
       c. Prepare bulletin announcements.
   3. The facilities coordinator
       a. Check with the program coordinator concerning audiovisual equipment, supplies, and classroom arrangements needed for the seminar.
       b. Arrange for health break items.
       c. Arrange for a public address system.
       d. Arrange for all supplies and materials to be at the seminar.

C. The stewardship commission will meet one month before the activity to review the accomplishment of all schedules and tasks.

D. The stewardship commission meets one week before the event to confirm all plans.

Step Two—Holding the Seminar

Step Three—Evaluation

Conduct an evaluation meeting of the commission to study the evaluation forms provided by the participants.

Step Four—Follow-up

Have teams available for follow-up work with those requesting help.

Stewardship

Outreach Idea Four:
Recycling Project
By Michael L. Roach

A community recycling effort spearheaded by your church is a way to express your concern for the environment. It can also double as a moneymaking activity for worthwhile community activities or projects. The recycling campaign can be publicized throughout the community through mass mailings, door-to-door canvassing, newspaper and radio ads, and telephoning. Encourage everyone in the congregation to involve a friend, relative, or neighbor.

Step One—Preliminary Planning
- A. Four months before the event the stewardship commission will meet
  1. Set a date and time for the collection effort to begin.
  2. Determine where the collected materials can be stored and picked up by recycling agencies.
  3. Schedule a second meeting in two weeks to begin finalizing plans.

- B. The stewardship commission will meet to assign various tasks to be completed.
  1. The program coordinator
     a. Develops the recycing schedule and logistics.
     b. Makes the final contact with the recycling agencies.
     c. Develops an evaluation form to be used at the conclusion of the project.

       d. Arranges for the storage and pick-up of recycled items.
  2. The publicity and promotion coordinator
       a. Develops a time line and plan of action for publicizing the project
       b. Prints materials to publicize the event and places newspaper and radio ads.
       c. Prepares bulletin announcements for your congregation as well as other local churches.
  3. The facilities coordinator
       a. Checks with the program coordinator concerning additional equipment and arrangements needed for the project.
       b. Arranges for refreshments and health-break items to be available on collection days for the volunteers.

C. The stewardship commission will meet one month before the activity to review the completion of all tasks and schedules.

D. The stewardship commission meets one week before the event to confirm all plans.

Step Two—Implementation

Kick off the environmental recycling effort.

Step Three—Evaluation

Hold an evaluation meeting of the commission to study the evaluation forms completed by the participants.